The status of sign languages in Europe

Report drawn up by
Ms Nina Timmermans
Consultant

in co-operation with the
Committee on the Rehabilitation and Integration
of People with disabilities (CD-P-RR)

Integration of people with disabilities

Council of Europe Publishing

French edition:

Le statut des langues des signes en Europe

ISBN 92-871-5723-5

Cover design: Graphic Design Workshop, Council of Europe
Layout: Desktop Publishing Unit, Council of Europe

Edited by Council of Europe Publishing
F-67075 Strasbourg Cedex
http://book.coe.int

ISBN 92-871-5720-0
© Council of Europe, April 2005
Printed at the Council of Europe

CONTENTS

PREFACE

The Council of Europe

The Council of Europe is a political organisation which was founded on 5 May 1949 by ten European countries in order to promote greater unity between its members. It now numbers 46 member states.

The main aims of the Organisation are to reinforce democracy, human rights and the rule of law and to develop common responses to political, social, cultural and legal challenges in its member states. Since 1989 the Council of Europe has integrated most of the countries of central and eastern Europe into its structures and supported them in their efforts to implement and consolidate their political, legal and administrative reforms.

The work of the Council of Europe has led, to date, to the adoption of almost 200 European conventions and agreements, which create the basis for a "common legal space" in Europe. They include the European Convention on Human Rights (1950), the European Cultural Convention (1954), the European Social Charter (1961), the European Convention on the Prevention of Torture (1987) and the Convention on Human Rights and Bioethics (1997). Numerous recommendations and resolutions of the Committee of Ministers propose policy guidelines for national governments.

The Partial Agreement in the Social and Public Health Field

Where a lesser number of member states of the Council of Europe wish to engage in some action in which not all their

European partners desire to join, they can conclude a 'Partial Agreement' which is binding on themselves alone.

The Partial Agreement in the Social and Public Health Field was concluded on this basis in 1959. At present, it has 18 member states.[1] Eight states participate as observers in the activities of the Committee on the Rehabilitation and Integration of People with disabilities.[2]

The principal areas of activity are:
- rehabilitation and integration of people with disabilities;
- protection of public health and especially the health of the consumer.

The activities in the disability area are supervised by the Committee on the Rehabilitation and Integration of People with disabilities and guided by the Coherent policy for people with disabilities, adopted by the Committee of Ministers of the Council of Europe in 1992 as Recommendation No. R (92) 6.

The Partial Agreement in the social and public health field is committed to upholding the rights of people with disabilities and advocates for their integration and full participation in society. Such a commitment should also be seen against the background of the European Convention on Human Rights and the European Social Charter, both major instruments of the Council of Europe.

Further information is available on the web site: www.coe.int/soc-sp

1. Austria, Belgium, Cyprus, Denmark, Finland, France, Germany, Ireland, Italy, Luxembourg, the Netherlands, Norway, Portugal, Slovenia, Spain, Sweden, Switzerland, the United Kingdom.
2. Estonia, Hungary, Iceland, Latvia, Lithuania, Poland, Romania, and Canada.

CHAPTER 1 – INTRODUCTION

1.1 About sign languages

Sign languages should not be confused with gesturing or "pantomime": they are natural languages in their own right, systematic and rule-based, with distinct lexicons (=vocabularies) of arbitrary signs (=conventional symbols) and grammatical structures (=system of rules) just as complex as spoken languages. Sign languages are languages that are conveyed by means of hand shapes, the movements of the hands and body, and the use of facial expressions and lip patterns. Whereas spoken languages use units of sounds to form words, sign languages use visual-gestural units of form, composed of four basic hand forms: hand shape (e.g. open or closed), hand location (e.g. on the middle of the forehead or in front of the chest), hand movement (e.g. upward or downward), and hand orientation (e.g. palm facing up or out).

Sign languages perform a similar range of functions to spoken languages: communicate, convey social relationships, express cultural identity, provide a source of delight through artistic forms of expression.

Sign language is not a universal language. Each country has its own national sign language. Some countries have more than one sign language, e.g. in Spain, Catalonian Sign Language is used in Catalonia, and Galician Sign Language in Galicia; in Belgium, Flemish Belgian Sign Language, Belgian French Sign Language, and German Sign Language are used; in Switzerland, Swiss-German, Swiss-French and Swiss-Italian Sign Language(s) are used; in Finland, Finnish Sign

Language and Finnish-Swedish Sign Language are used. Most sign languages are mutually unintelligible.

Sign languages do not have the same vocabulary or syntax as the spoken languages of the same geographical area. They are independent from the spoken languages around them and have evolved in the deaf communities (endogenous languages). For example, unlike the spoken languages, American Sign Language (ASL) has more in common with French Sign Languages (LSF) than with British Sign Language (BSL), the reason being as follows. The first school for the deaf was established in Paris during the eighteenth century, where teachers taught French Sign Language (LSF). In 1816 American educator Thomas Gallaudet travelled to Paris to study the French method of teaching. He returned to the United States with the deaf teacher Laurent Clerc and together they opened the first American school for the deaf in Hartford, Connecticut, in 1817. They adopted the French signing method for use in American classrooms. The merger of French signs with signs used by American deaf people at that time formed what is now called American Sign Language (ASL).

However, similar to spoken languages, sign languages exhibit the same types of variation: variations according to region, social or ethic group, social situation, age, and gender. Like spoken languages, sign languages do evolve.

Sign languages are the first or preferred language for many people for many prelingually deaf people and some hearing people who grow up with deaf family members. People who are deafened or hard of hearing usually have a spoken language as their first or preferred language. However, they may chose to learn sign languages to ease communication.

1.2 About this report

On 15 February 2001, the Committee of Ministers of the Council of Europe assigned ad hoc terms of reference to the Committee on the Rehabilitation and Integration of People with disabilities (Partial Agreement) (CD-P-RR) to draw up an opinion on Parliamentary Assembly Recommendation 1492 (2001), in particular on paragraph 12. xiii concerning sign languages.

In its opinion, the CD-P-RR considered drafting a report concerning the official recognition and the status of sign languages in the member and observer states of the Partial Agreement in the Social and Public Health Field. That commitment formed the origin of the present report, which gives an overview of the status of sign languages in 26 Council of Europe member states (18 members of and 8 observers to the Partial Agreement in the Social and Public Health Field).

This report is a timely initiative. It could serve as the starting point of a wider study of the needs of sign language users in Council of Europe member states. Reference to such a needs analysis is made both in Recommendation 1598 (2003) of the Parliamentary Assembly of the Council of Europe "Protection of sign languages in the member states of the Council of Europe" and the reply of the Committee of Ministers thereto (c.f. Appendices 3 and 4). Such a study could, in turn, form the basis for any debate on a possible future Council of Europe legal instrument to protect the sign languages and the rights of their users.

The information in the present report is based on:

- the European Union of the Deaf (EUD) Paper "Update on the status of sign languages in the European Union", March 2001;

- the comments to the EUD paper received by the CD-P-RR from delegations of Belgium, Cyprus, Finland, Lithuania, the Netherlands, Norway, Poland, Spain, Slovenia, Sweden, Switzerland (2001-2002);

- the comments to the first draft report (P-SG (2003)) 15 of 31 July 2003 received by the CD-P-RR from delegations of the Czech Republic, Germany, Hungary, Luxembourg, Switzerland and the United Kingdom.

11

- the Council of Europe report "Rehabilitation and integration of people with disabilities: policy and legislation", 6th edition, February 2002;
- the Council of Europe report "Rehabilitation and integration of people with disabilities: policy and legislation", 7th edition, April 2003;
- the UN report "Government Action on Disability Policy, a Global Survey", 1997;
- the UN report "Government Implementation of the Standard Rules As Seen By Member Organizations of World Federation of the Deaf – WFD", 1997;
- the UN report "Government Implementation of the Standard Rules As Seen By Member Organizations of Rehabilitation International – RI", 1997;
- information on EUD's website www.eudnet.org;
- information on Disability World's website www.disabilityworld.com;

The status (signing, ratification or entry into force) of the European Charter for Regional or Minority Languages is indicated in a footnote (status as of 25 January 2005).

CHAPTER 2 – HISTORICAL BACKGROUND

2.1. European Parliament resolutions

It could be argued that the European Parliament was the first actor addressing the issue of sign languages at European level. Its resolution of 1988 still remains valid in many areas and on several issues which were raised at that time. Yet, due to the lack of progress made, as perceived by the deaf community, pressure increased in the 1990s and led to the adoption of the resolution of 1998, exactly ten years after the first instrument. The following chapter summarises the issues raised in both texts.

2.1.1. European Parliament Resolution on Sign Languages for Deaf People (1988)

The European Parliament called on the Commission to make a proposal to the Council concerning the official recognition of the sign language used by deaf people in each member state. It called upon the member states to abolish any remaining obstacles to the use of sign languages.

The European Parliament stressed the importance of recognising sign language interpreting as a profession and of establishing full-time sign language interpreter training and employment programmes in each member state under the responsibility of the national associations for the deaf. It urged member states to submit, in consultation with the European Regional Secretariat of the World Federation of the Deaf (WFD), projects for the training of sufficient numbers of sign language tutors, assessors and interpreters, as well as for support under the European Social Fund. The European Parliament called upon Community institutions to set an example by making provision, as a matter of principle, for sign language interpretation at meetings organised under their auspices and attended by deaf people.

The European Parliament called upon broadcasting authorities to include translation into sign language, or at least subtitles, of television news programmes, those of political interest and, to the extent possible, of a selection of cultural and general interest programmes. It also urged broadcasting authorities, in consultation with the European Regional Secretariat for the Deaf and the European Broadcasting Union, to determine minimum levels of provision of sign language interpretation, sub-titling and teletext for programmes aimed at adults and children.

It urged member states to ensure that all relevant government circulars on welfare benefits, health and employment are produced using sign languages on video for the use of the deaf community. It called upon the European Commission to support research in the area of television services for the deaf.

It called upon member states, in co-operation with the European Commission, to support pilot projects aimed at teaching sign languages to hearing children and adults, using deaf people trained for the purpose and to back research in this area.

It urged member states to support research into and publication of up-to-date dictionaries of their respective national sign languages and invited the European Commission to foster such activities, and to promote development of multilingual dictionaries of the sign languages in use within the Community in due course.

It invited the Commission to consider how, at a suitable juncture, community-level exchanges might best be brought about between those proficient in their respective countries' sign languages and cultures.

Finally, the European Parliament considered it essential that deaf people be fully involved in determining policy for the non-hearing at national and Community level, notably through the European Regional Secretariat of the WFD, and called for more generous funding under the Community budget for development of devices for deaf people in the member states.

2.1.2. European Parliament Resolution on Sign Languages (1998)

The European Parliament called on the European Commission to make a proposal to the Council concerning official recognition of the sign language used by deaf people in each member state, and to ensure EU funding programmes in the field of education and employment training including training of sign language tutors and interpreters.

It called on the Commission to ensure that all EU programmes are accessible to deaf people and recognition is given to the need for sign language interpretation and to introduce measures on deaf awareness training for officials working in EU institutions. It called on the Commission and the member states to ensure that public meetings organised by EU institutions are accessible to deaf people by providing sign language interpretation service on request.

It called on the Commission to examine, in the context of public service television, the possibility of introducing legislation enabling the translation into sign language, or at least the subtitling of news broadcasts, programmes of political interest – especially during election campaigns – and, as far as possible, of cultural and general interest programmes.

Finally, the European Parliament called on the Commission to introduce a proposal for framework legislation to ensure compatibility of telecommunications text and videophone equipment for deaf people across Europe, and to introduce measures to ensure universal design in multimedia applications so that deaf people are not excluded from new applications, and, in addition, to undertake studies concerning other audiovisual services for deaf people.

2.2. The European Charter for Regional or Minority Languages (1992)

For many years various bodies within the Council of Europe have been expressing concern over the situation of regional or minority languages. It is true that the Convention for the Protection of Human Rights and Fundamental Freedoms in its Article 14 lays down the principle of non-discrimination, in particular outlawing, at least with respect to the enjoyment of the rights and freedoms guaranteed by the Convention, any discrimination based on such grounds as language or association with a national minority.

Important as this is, however, it only creates a right for individuals not to be subjected to discrimination, but not a system of positive protection for minority languages and the communities using them, as was pointed out by the then called Consultative Assembly of the Council of Europe as early as 1957 in its Resolution 136. In 1961, the by then renamed Parliamentary Assembly of the Council of Europe called for a protection measure to supplement the European Convention to be devised in order to safeguard the rights of minorities to enjoy their own culture, to use their own language, to establish their own schools and so on (Recommendation 285).

For the purposes of the Charter:[1]

  a. "*regional or minority languages*" means languages that are:

   i. traditionally used within a given territory of a state by nationals of that state who form a group numerically smaller than the rest of the state's population; and

   ii. different from the official language(s) of that state; excluding dialects of the official language(s) of the state or the languages of migrants;

  b. "*territory in which the regional or minority language is used*" means the geographical area in which the said language is the

---

1. See Article 1. Emphasis added by the author.

mode of expression of a number of people justifying the adoption of the various protective and promotional measures provided for in the Charter;

c. *"non-territorial languages"* means languages used by nationals of the state which differ from the language or languages used by the rest of the state's population but which, although traditionally used within the territory of the state, cannot be identified with a particular area thereof.

As is made clear in its preamble, the Charter's overriding purpose is cultural. It is designed to protect and promote regional or minority languages as a threatened aspect of Europe's cultural heritage.[1] For this reason it not only contains a non-discrimination clause concerning the use of these languages but also provides for measures offering active support for them: the aim is to ensure, as far as reasonably possible, the use of regional or minority languages in education and the media and to permit their use in judicial and administrative settings, economic and social life, and cultural activities. Only in this way can such languages be compensated, where necessary, for unfavourable conditions in the past, preserved and developed as a living facet of Europe's cultural identity.

The Charter sets out to protect and promote regional or minority languages, not linguistic minorities.[2] For this reason emphasis is placed on the cultural dimension and the use of a regional or minority language in all aspects of the life of its speakers. The Charter does not establish any individual or collective rights for the speakers of regional or minority languages. Nevertheless, the obligations of the parties with regard to the status of these languages and the domestic legislation which will have to be introduced in compliance with the charter will have an obvious effect on the situation of the communities concerned and their individual members.

---

1. Emphasis added by the author.
2. Emphasis added by the author.

2.3. Flensburg Recommendations on the Implementation of Policy Measures for Regional or Minority Languages (2000)

With support from the European Commission, and in close co-operation with the Council of Europe and the European Bureau for Lesser Used Languages, the European Centre for Minority Issues (ECMI), Flensburg, Germany, organised, on 23 and 24 June 2000, an international conference on "Evaluating policy measures for minority languages in Europe: Towards effective, cost-effective and democratic implementation". Participants included noted scholars in minority issues, representatives from major international organisations, non-governmental organisations, and member countries of the Council of Europe. The conference was an important element in a larger project on the analysis of policies adopted in favour of minority languages, particularly, but not exclusively, in the context of the European Charter for Regional or Minority Languages.

The European Charter for Regional or Minority Languages is a novel instrument in international law, because its focus is not on the rights of minorities, but on languages themselves. Hence, in the conference convened by ECMI, legal standards were taken as given, with debates emphasising instead issues of implementation.

Owing to the extreme degree of variability of situations between different regional or minority languages (and, of course, between the states in which these regional or minority languages are traditionally used), the purpose of the conference was not to make general recommendations regarding the set of specific measures that should be adopted in order to protect or revitalise these languages. Accordingly, the conference focused not on the specific measures that should be adopted by states (whether such measures are adopted explicitly in order to comply with Charter obligations or not), but on how authorities at various levels choose policy measures in favour of regional or minority languages, because some very practical issues of decision-making arise in all cases. More precisely, emphasis was placed on how states can meet principles of good public policy, in particular aiming at: (i) effective policies; (ii) cost-effective policies; and (iii) democratic policies.

The concepts of effectiveness and cost-effectiveness, as well as the characteristics of genuinely democratic policies in the context of language policy implementation, were discussed at length during the conference, generating consensus around the view that effectiveness, cost-effectiveness and democracy are among the core principles of "good practice".

The recommendations emanating from the conference are intended to draw attention to relevant principles in the selection, design, implementation and evaluation of policies in favour of regional or minority languages. They also assist authorities in implementing the Charter, with a view to helping states that have not yet ratified (or signed) the Charter, in assessing the practical implications of doing so, and in offering assistance to other organisations, particularly NGOs, involved in minority language policies.

With regard to sign languages, the ECMI has formulated the following recommendation:

"Due recognition should also be given to Sign Languages. The Council of Europe and other international organisations should consider the desirability and feasibility of preparing a legal instrument to safeguard these languages and the rights of their users. Likewise, the European Commission is requested to sympathetically consider the inclusion of actions to support Sign Languages in their language programmes."

2.4. Parliamentary Assembly Recommendation 1492 (2001) on the rights of national minorities

On 23 January 2001 the Parliamentary Assembly of the Council of Europe adopted Recommendation 1492 (2001) on the rights of national minorities. In paragraph 12. xiii of the

Recommendation, the Parliamentary Assembly recommends that the Committee of Ministers gives the various sign languages utilised in Europe a protection similar to that afforded by the European Charter for Regional or Minority Languages, possibly by means of the adoption of a recommendation to member states.

The text of Recommendation 1492 (2001)[1] was examined by the Committee of Ministers (Ministers' Deputies) on 15 February 2001, who decided to assign ad hoc terms of reference to the Committee on the Rehabilitation and Integration of People with disabilities (Partial Agreement) (CD-P-RR) to draw up an opinion on that recommendation, in particular on paragraph 12. xiii concerning sign languages.

Opinion of the Committee on the Rehabilitation and Integration of People with disabilities (Partial Agreement) (CD-P-RR)

The Committee on the Rehabilitation and Integration of People with disabilities (Partial Agreement) (CD-P-RR) considers that sign languages can, in principle, be regarded as non-territorial languages. It is pertinent to note that sign languages meet the definition criteria of non-territorial languages as set out in the European Charter for Minority or Regional Languages, i.e. "Languages used by nationals of the state which differ from the language or languages used by the rest of the state's population but which, although traditionally used within the territory of the state, cannot be identified with a particular area thereof." (Part I, Article 1c.)

Sign languages are typically used throughout the country of which they are native: British Sign Language in Great Britain, French Sign Language in France, German Sign Language in Germany, Italian Sign Language in Italy, etc. However, it is worth noting that in some countries more than one sign language may exist. These sign languages are used in certain geographical areas only and thus meet the definition of regional minority languages. For example: in Spain,

---

1. The text of the Recommendation is set out in Appendix I to this report.

Catalonian Sign Language is used in Catalonia, and Galician sign Language in Galicia; in Belgium, Flemish Belgian Sign Language, Belgian French Sign Language, and German Sign Language are used; in Switzerland, Swiss-German, Swiss-French and Swiss-Italian Sign Language(s) are used; in Finland, Finnish Sign Language and Finnish-Swedish Sign Language are used.

Furthermore, sign language users are a cultural and linguistic minority. In relation to the European Parliament Resolution on sign languages of 18 November 1998, the CD-P-RR considers that every one of the different sign languages used in Europe has its specific cultural identity. In accordance with the Council of Europe Declaration on cultural diversity, adopted by the Committee of Ministers on 7 December 2000, member states should develop and/or maintain measures to sustain, protect and promote linguistic and cultural diversity, in order to enhance pluralism and multi-cultural societies in Europe. Also sign languages should be recognised as an expression of cultural wealth. They constitute an important element of Europe's linguistic and cultural heritage.

In conclusion, the CD-P-RR welcomes the Parliamentary Assembly Recommendation as a further substantial step in securing human rights and dignity, full citizenship and active participation in the life of the community for all people with disabilities. Pursuant to the Flensburg Recommendations on the implementation of policy measures for regional or minority languages, issued by the European Centre for Minority Issues (ECMI) in June 2000, the CD-P-RR recommends that the Council of Europe should prepare a legal instrument to safeguard sign languages and the rights of their users and in particular to promote the individual right to the general use of sign languages and facilitating that use by a co-ordinated set of measures deemed most appropriate, reflecting the variety of instruments, policies and practices in member states.

In this connection, some delegations expressed themselves in favour of recommending the elaboration of an additional protocol on sign languages to the European Charter for Regional or Minority Languages.

Concerning the official recognition of sign languages at national level, the CD-P-RR could consider drafting a report for the attention of the Parliamentary Assembly on the status of sign languages in member states.[1]

Opinion of the Committee of Experts of the European Charter for Regional or Minority Languages

The Committee of Experts of the European Charter for Regional or Minority Languages points out that the protection provided by the Charter is specifically designed for those languages defined in its Article 1, that is languages that are "traditionally used within a given territory of a State by nationals of that State..." and "different from the official language(s) of the State". It does not include the dialects of the official language(s) and the languages of migrants. The Charter may also be applied to less widely used official languages (Article 3).

Thus the authors of the Charter, in adopting these formulations, limited the application of the Charter to certain categories of languages.

According to the Committee of Experts this limitation by no means implies that the languages of migrants or sign languages should not receive an appropriate form of protection. As for sign languages, it should be recognised that the Charter was not conceived to meet their specific needs. Sign languages are present in all European states and they are not currently the subject of a special international instrument addressing their particular needs, whether from a social, cultural or human rights perspective. The Committee of Experts stated that it would welcome an initiative aiming to promote and protect sign languages through a separate instrument that would take into account the special situation and needs of the users of these languages.

---

1. The present report was initiated by that commitment.

22

Committee of Ministers' reply to Parliamentary Assembly Recommendation 1492 (2001)

On 13 June 2002 the Committee of Ministers adopted its reply to Parliamentary Assembly Recommendation 1492 (2001), including the integral opinions of the Committee on the Rehabilitation and Integration of People with disabilities (CD-P-RR) and the Committee of Experts of the European Charter for Regional or Minority Languages opinion in Appendices to that reply.[1]

2.5. Parliamentary Assembly Recommendation 1598 (2003) on the protection of sign languages in the member states of the Council of Europe

On 1 April 2003, the Parliamentary Assembly of the Council of Europe adopted Recommendation 1598 (2003) on the protection of sign languages in the member states of the Council of Europe.[2] The Assembly recognises sign languages as the expression of Europe's cultural wealth and as a feature of Europe's linguistic and cultural heritage. The Assembly also recognises sign languages as a complete and natural means of communication for deaf people and takes the view that official recognition of these languages will help deaf people to become integrated into society and gain access to education, employment and justice.

The Assembly recommends to the Committee of Ministers to devise a specific legal instrument on the rights of sign language users, and accordingly:

– to instruct the relevant bodies of the Council of Europe to undertake a preparatory study in consultation with national experts and representatives of the deaf community in order to clarify outstanding issues in regard to the protection of the use of sign languages;

---

1. The text of that reply is set out in Appendix II to this report.
2. The text of that Recommendation is set out in Appendix III to this report.

– to define clear goals to be achieved, exact deadlines to be met, and resources and methods to be used, founded on a full study of requirements with the mandatory participation of associations representing the users of these languages;

– to consider drafting an additional protocol to the European Charter for Regional or Minority Languages incorporating sign languages into the charter, among the non-territorial minority languages.

On 16 April 2003, the Committee of Ministers (Ministers' Deputies) examined Recommendation 1598 (2003) of the Parliamentary Assembly and decided to communicate it, amongst others, to the Committee on the Rehabilitation and Integration of People with disabilities (CD-P-RR) for information and possible comments.

Opinion of the Committee on the Rehabilitation and Integration of People with disabilities (CD-P-RR)

In its Opinion adopted in writing on 10 October 2003, the CD-P-RR notes with satisfaction that the Parliamentary Assembly referred to its opinion of 28 February 2002 on Recommendation 1492 (2001), of which the Committee of Ministers had taken note and appended to its reply of 13 June 2002. The CD-P-RR holds the view that the considerations included in that opinion are still valid and applicable.

The CD-P-RR wishes to recall that it launched the process of drafting a report on the status of sign languages in its member and observer states at its 24th session, and agrees to further pursue the issue of that comparative analysis on the status of sign languages in its member and observer states.

The Committee offers to contribute its multidisciplinary expertise to the drafting of any future Council of Europe legal instrument concerning the protection of sign languages and the rights of their users, of which the exact modalities and details regarding the process and the content remain yet to be specified.

Committee of Ministers' reply to Parliamentary Assembly Recommendation 1598 (2003)

On 16 June 2004, the Committee of Ministers of the Council of Europe adopted its reply to Parliamentary Assembly Recommendation 1598 (2003), in which it concluded that sign languages merited special consideration and protection. As to the question of a possible future Council of Europe instrument, the reply states that a study of the needs of sign language users should be conducted first, and that the current report could form a good basis for that needs analysis.[1]

1. The text of that reply is set out in Appendix IV.

CHAPTER 3 – THE STATUS OF SIGN LANGUAGES IN MEMBER STATES OF THE PARTIAL AGREEMENT IN THE SOCIAL AND PUBLIC HEALTH FIELD

3.1. Austria[1]

Sign language is recognised as the main means of communication between deaf persons and others. There are government measures to encourage media and other forms of public information for making their services accessible to persons with disabilities. Examples are: telephone amplifiers for hearing impaired persons and no telephone charges for deaf persons with a specific telephone set.[2] Aids for communication are possible for people with sensory disabilities. All supplementary equipment needed by deaf people for their vocational and private life can be subsidised as can technical equipment. If a deaf person needs a sign language interpreter for essential business (e.g. at an authority, an important contract, a difficult medical investigation) there are benefits to cover the cost.[3]

3.2. Belgium[4]

3.2.1. Flanders

Flemish Sign Language Centre (VGTC)

While participating in the Sign Languages Project of the European Union of the Deaf in 1997, the Flemish National

---

1. In Austria, the European Charter for Regional or Minority Languages (1992) entered into force on 1 October 2001.
2. Government Action on Disability Policy, A Global Survey, Dimitris Michailakis, 1997.
3. Rehabilitation and integration of people with disabilities: policy and legislation, 7th edition (2003), Council of Europe Publishing.
4. Belgium has not signed The European Charter for Regional or Minority Languages (1992).

Commission brought together experts in several areas, such as linguistics, Flemish Sign Language users, schools for the deaf, and parents associations. After the Sign Languages Project came to an end, Fevlado (*Federatie van Vlaamse Doven Organisaties*) decided to try to maintain the intellectual values and know-how that had been developed. As a result, Fevlado set up the Flemish Sign Language Centre that has continued the research work on Flemish Sign Language. The Centre also supports contacts with schools for the deaf, developing sign language teaching, and promoting sign language research at academic level.

School for deaf and hard of hearing children in Brussels-Berchem

Following the initiative of some teachers of the deaf at the Kasterlinden School for the deaf in Brussels, Fevlado set up a new school "'t Signaal" in 1997. This organisation monitors and co-ordinates an experimental pilot project in bilingual teaching. The project aims to teach deaf children using a twin-teachers approach. This means that the hearing official teacher is supported by a deaf assistant, who teaches lessons through Flemish Sign Language. The objective of Fevlado is to keep this experiment running and to secure funding to expand this approach to several schools/classes. The main problem is that there are not enough qualified deaf teachers (though now there are a few students undertaking university level training to become officially recognised teachers).

Attitude of schools for the deaf towards Flemish Sign Language

Before 1997, schools for the deaf considered Flemish Sign Language to be the last resort in the teaching of deaf children. It was only used where an oral approach to education did not provide adequate results. Since the Sign Languages Project, a change has occurred in how the schools for the deaf view Flemish Sign Language: it is now seen as a valuable means for teaching deaf children. Parents can choose an oral education or an education delivered through Flemish Sign

Language. Schools for the deaf are now working with Fevlado to improve their teaching programmes, to use the appropriate Flemish Sign Language vocabulary and grammar, to find appropriate deaf people to work in schools for the deaf as assistants, and so on. Fevlado is currently running a project, sponsored by the King Baudouin Foundation, in partnership with the schools for the deaf in Flanders and the Sign Language Centre to develop sign vocabulary for concepts for which there is no Flemish Sign Language vocabulary available yet.

Legal Change: Resolution of 5 May 1999 of the Flemish Government

After the Sign Languages Project, Fevlado has continued its work at political level using the results of the Sign Languages Project in a positive way. Fevlado's lobbying brought them into contact with a very diverse group of politicians from several political parties.

The Flemish Parliament voted to support the resolution on 5 May 1999. This resolution asked the government to take the necessary measures to improve the situation of deaf people in Flanders. The Minister of Welfare in Flanders has adopted this resolution into her work programme and asked her administration to work out several steps for the practical application of this resolution. The ministry is working very closely with Fevlado, along with schools for the deaf and services for deaf people. One of the points explicitly mentioned in the resolution is the establishment of a commission to prepare for the official recognition of Flemish Sign Language in Flanders.

Sign Language Research in Flanders

Research projects on the status of Flemish Sign Language (1998), the various dialects (with a view of standardisation) and the perception of sign language (2003) in educational institutions (2003) have recently been conducted and the results have been published. Researchers included deaf researchers and members of Fevlado.

TV Broadcasting

In 1998 Fevlado had its own TV-series, "World of Signs" (26 broadcastings of 20 minutes), which was repeated in 1999. This initiative aimed at providing the hearing community in Flanders with a better understanding of Flemish deaf people and their sign language.

Sign Language Interpreters

Flemish Sign Language interpreters are now better paid by the government (due to the joint lobbying of Fevlado and CAB, the Flemish Sign Language Interpreting Bureau). As a result, deaf people in Flanders now have more hours allocated to them for use of Flemish Sign Language interpreters. Training for Flemish Sign Language interpreters is improving, but the problem remains that interpreter training is still only available in "evening-class" format.

With the aim of providing a high-level education for the Flemish Sign Language interpreters, Fevlado has been in contact with the Antwerp High School for Social Studies to set up a specific training programme for Flemish Sign Language interpreters. This will be a full-time, daytime programme.

Comments of the Flemish Community in Belgium

Under its "inclusive" policy, the Flemish Community has developed a project (*"Teletolk Vlaanderen"* = tele-interpretation for the Flemish region) aimed at making it easier for the deaf or hard of hearing to communicate over the telephone. The project is a sign that the Flemish Community is committed to promoting communication not only between people who are hard of hearing but also between people who are deaf or hard of hearing and people with no hearing impairments.

The Flemish Community considers that although more could be done, assuming more interpreters can be found, the measures already taken in favour of people with disabilities, in particular to cover the cost of technical aids and provide the assistance of sign-language interpreters as well as education support for children who are deaf or hard of hearing, are forms of practical, immediate-impact support that should make it easier for deaf and hearing-impaired people to take up their place in society. From a legal standpoint, these regulatory measures laid down in decrees adopted by the Flemish government establish the subjective right of people who are deaf or hard of hearing to receive financial support and to claim this right before the appropriate courts of law, providing they meet the statutory requirements for receipt of such support.

The steps already taken in this field by the Flemish authorities are a sign of their awareness of, and commitment to the cause of people who are deaf or hearing-impaired who enjoy fundamental rights under Article 13 of the EC Treaty which guarantees protection against all forms of discrimination against people with disabilities. Seen in this context, the need for an additional protocol to the European Charter for Regional or Minority Languages or other common European legal approaches are a matter of less urgency for the Flemish Community than the generally acknowledged need to focus attention in the policy sphere on the many measures already in place to enable people who are deaf or hard of hearing to communicate or to make their communication easier.

3.2.2. Walloon and Region of Brussels-Capital

Legislation and status of sign language

On 25 November 2003, the Belgian *Moniteur* published the text of a Decree dated 22 October 2003 on the recognition of sign language. Article 1 of the Decree provides "that the sign language of French-speaking Belgium shall be recognised, and this language shall be the language of visual gesture specific to the hearing-impaired population of the French-speaking Community". Article 2 of that Decree set up an advisory board on sign language with the function of submitting to the government, of its own motion or on request, opinions and proposals on all issues relating to the use of sign language.

Education and teaching by deaf teachers

In the field of special education, little has changed since the 1996-97 report. Mainstream education, however, has seen real progress on a legal level since the former Education Minister launched her decree on immersion. Amendments to the project proposed by the FFSB (*Fédération Francophone des Sourds de Belgique*), working together with the APEDAF (*Association de Parents d'Enfants Déficients Auditifs*, Association of Parents of Hearing-Deficient Children), enabled Belgian-French Sign Language to be recognised as a medium for teaching in schools, on a par with spoken languages such as Flemish, English or Spanish.

Since September 2000, an infants' class in Namur has been offering courses taught in Belgian-French Sign Language to both deaf and hearing children, but it is the parents of the deaf children who contribute financially. In the French-speaking community there are currently four special schools for deaf children.

Financing and training of interpreters

As regards the French-speaking Community Commission of the Region of Brussels-Capital, by decree of 27 April 1995 the deaf have the right to signed interpretation. In the Brussels Capital region, the SISB (*Service d'Interprétation pour Sourds de Bruxelles,* Brussels Interpretation Service for the Deaf) has been recognised since 1 July 2000 as a service. In this way, every deaf or hearing-impaired person entitled to benefit from the regulations of the Brussels French-speaking Service for the Disabled can make an annual request to the non-profit organisation Info-sourds (which has French-speaking Community Commission accreditation as an interpretation service for the deaf) for a maximum of 30 non-transferable index-linked tickets. Info-sourds undertakes to distribute tickets, each valid for an hour's interpretation, to those concerned and provides them with an up-to-date list of approved interpreters, with information about each interpreter's fields of competence. The interpreter returns the tickets received to the organisation, which reimburses him/her for their value.

The tasks of this interpretation service for the deaf are as follows:

- to draw up a list of interpreters using sign language or providing any other assistance with communication; this list is approved by the college. Only these interpreters are recognised as eligible to provide interpretation which the Brussels Service will reimburse;

- to draw up a contract with each interpreter guaranteeing the deaf a quality service at a fixed price;

- to arrange ongoing training for interpreters;

- to act as intermediary between the deaf and interpreters;

- to process interpretation requests from deaf people through a central office.

Grants are awarded to the interpretation service to cover staff and operational costs.

In the region of Walloon, the SISW (*Service d'Interprétation pour Sourds de Wallonie,* Walloon Interpretation Service for the Deaf), a non-profit organisation established in 1995 and based in Namur, is still not officially recognised, but is financed entirely by the Ministry of Social Affairs of the Region of Walloon. The delay in recognition is due to the fact that the parties concerned are still looking for a better system that will give more flexibility in the number of hours granted.

As needs differ so much from one deaf person to another, the FFSB insists on preserving a demand-based system. In addition to administrative staff responsible for its daily running and the processing of requests for interpretation, the SISW team consists of staff interpreters and contracted freelance interpreters. The SISW handles requests for interpretation in all areas of social and professional life. Access to the service costs a fee of 12.39 euros every six months. Interpretation is provided free to private individuals, but a charge is made for business users. In an average year the SISW receives some 1,200 requests, to roughly 80% of which it is able to respond.

Sign language at school

In the school sector, interpretation is still managed by the Ministry of Health – which specifies speech therapy as a pre-requisite condition – and not by the Ministry of Education. At present, LPC (*Langue Parlée Complétée,* Complete Spoken Language) and AKA are the most widely used systems, to the detriment of Sign Language. In certain public institutions the personnel learn sign language, but the numbers are still very small. At present, interpreters come mainly from the Promotion Sociale courses organised by the administrators of Belgium's French-speaking Community.

Television

Since 1981, RTBF (*Radio Télévision Belge Francophone,* Belgium's French-speaking state channel) has been providing sign language interpretation of the 7.30 evening news, but it is frequently cancelled in favour of live sports coverage. Since 1999, French-speaking Community funding has enabled RTBF to create 2 1/2 full-time posts for closed-sub-title coding of some programmes. The FFSB conducted a survey to determine which programmes should be subtitled. However, the most-requested programme is only subtitled 50% of the time (one programme in two).

RTBF's new children's news programme Niouzz is translated into Belgian-French Sign Language, but only on its fourth and last broadcast at 11a.m the next day. The RTBF broadcasts *Tu vois ce que je veux dire* ('You see what I mean') 6 to 8 times a year. Created by and for the deaf, the programme has been running since 1995. It is created by a volunteer camera crew – 3 deaf and 3 hearing. RTBF takes responsibility for editing, subtitling, and broadcasting.

Training for parents

The French-speaking Community's *Promotion Sociale* system offers Belgian-French Sign Language courses, but these are often unsuited to parents' needs, particularly as not many parents have access to the reduction of working hours that is normally part of the *Promotion Sociale* package.

However, the courses are very popular and many institutions include Belgian-French Sign Language as one of their courses. One consequence of this, in view of the lack of qualified deaf teachers, is that the system engages deaf persons with no basic training in language teaching. FFSB is unable to intervene with the organising bodies of these institutions. More and more parents meet the deaf community in order to familiarise themselves with deaf culture and Belgian-French Sign Language but many others opt for PLC, which is much easier to learn.

3.2.3. German-speaking Community

Sign language for deaf people has no officially recognised status. There are no government measures to encourage media to make their services accessible for persons with disabilities but there are government measures to make other forms of public information services available. The following service is provided in order to facilitate information and communication: sign language interpretation being available for any purpose.[1]

In the German-speaking Community, hearing-impaired individuals with an adequate understanding of sign language can benefit from French signed interpretation provided by the SISW under the terms described in connection with the French-speaking Community. For interpretation in German Sign Language, those concerned are eligible to between 15 and 30 hours per year with trained freelance interpreters or services for the deaf and hearing-impaired in Germany. The Office for the Disabled subsidises this service up to 80% but little use is made of this arrangement. Subsidies for special materials contribute to the integration of those concerned. Services on offer in the areas of personal assistance, training,

---

1. Country report on Rule 5 "Accessibility" of the UN Standard Rules on the Equalization of Opportunities for Persons with Disabilities.

employment and leisure complement efforts to encourage self-sufficiency and improve beneficiaries' quality of life.

3.3. Cyprus[1]

Sign language in the education of hearing-impaired persons

The education of hearing-impaired students in Cyprus, since the establishment of the School for the Deaf in 1953, has been based on the oral method accompanied by natural gestures and body language when necessary. At the beginning of the 1990s, radical changes in the education of hearing-impaired persons occurred in Cyprus. The Ministry of Education and Culture adopted the policy of inclusion of children with special needs in regular education, a practice that was legislated in 1999. As a result, the vast majority of hearing-impaired students are mainstreamed, attending regular schools, from preschool to tertiary education, and only a small number of them still attend the School for the Deaf.

Sign language is not used in the mainstream, which is a pure auditory-oral school setting. However, specialised teachers who support hearing impaired students in the mainstream may employ natural gestures and body language for more effective communication with their students. At the School for the Deaf, the oral method is still in use but it has become more flexible by using more free and open modes of communication based on the philosophy of Total Communication, a method that includes sign language and is used at the School for the Deaf mainly with students who failed to become oral or their prospects to become oral are poor. Nevertheless, the issue of training of the teachers of hearing-impaired students to become skillful signers still exists.

---

1. In Cyprus, the European Charter for Regional or Minority Languages (1992) entered into force on 1 December 2002.

Sign language and deaf adults

Adult deaf people have given the most impulsion in the promotion and use of sign language as an effective mode of communication.

The impact on deaf adults in Cyprus of the trend in Europe and the USA for sign language to be recognised as a linguistically complete and therefore autonomous language, on the one hand, and the recognition of the right of the deaf to have and use their own language within their own culture, on the other hand, has been strong enough to raise their self-awareness and enable them to feel positively about sign language.

The systematic efforts by the organisations of the deaf and the accession of Cyprus to the European Union have increased the interest in sign language at various levels, and now the situation is as follows:

A bulletin broadcasted by C.B.C. is translated into sign language. A request to the C.B.C. for a separate bulletin for the deaf has been submitted.

The Pancyprian Organisation of Deaf Persons organises sign language lessons for deaf and hearing persons and financial assistance for these persons is given by the Ministry of Labour and Social Insurance. Similar lessons are offered by the Ministry of Education and Culture within the framework of the programme of further education.

Interpretation into sign language is secured for deaf persons who have to present themselves to court, or participate in seminars.

Furthermore, the organisations of the deaf demand from the Cyprus Government to recognise, by legislation, the Cyprus Sign Language as the official language of the deaf.

General remarks

The Cyprus Sign Language is currently in a transitional stage. It received and continues to receive strong influences mainly from the American Sign Language and the Greek Sign

Language. It is a fact that the Cyprus Sign Language linguistically is steadily being enriched and upgraded. Although it has not yet become a fully developed language, it appears to be in the dynamics of becoming an effective mode of communication, especially for the adult deaf. It also appears to be the central constituent of the emerging concept of Cyprus Deaf Culture.

3.4. Denmark[1]

Social interpretation project

In a three and a half year project from 2000-2003, deaf people had the right to sign language interpretation free of charge in situations where they previously had to pay themselves. Danish Sign Language interpretation was free:

- when visiting the doctor, dentist, chiropractor, physiotherapist, etc.;

- during conversations with a "home-help", lawyer, insurance company, etc.;

- in education (evening classes, open university, etc.);

- when receiving treatment in private hospitals;

- at cultural events;

- at meetings with unions and others within the labour market;

- at private events, leisure activities, lectures, etc.

Danish Sign Language interpreter training

In 1998 the Danish Sign Language interpreter training was extended to three and a half years. The first year focuses on providing basic Danish Sign Language input. In principle, this is open to everybody.

---

1. In Denmark, the European Charter for Regional or Minority Languages (1992) entered into force on 1 January 2001.

Deaf teacher education

There is a working group focusing on deaf teacher education. It proposed that more and better education be made available to deaf teachers. This proposal is being considered by the Association of County Councils in Denmark.

Danish Sign Language training for parents

The parents' association "Bonaventure" has planned a training programme for parents in conjunction with the Ministry of Education.

Danish Sign Language dictionary

In 1999, preliminary work began on a new, extended Dictionary of Danish Sign Language. A steering committee was formed, working in co-operation with a linguist.

Cover of expenses for sign language interpretation

In special cases the health care reimbursement scheme will pay the costs incurred by interpreter assistance. If the individual doctor finds it necessary to request the assistance of an interpreter to be able to finish a treatment/examination the doctor may do so without any expense for the citizen. This may be necessary both in the case of deaf/hard of hearing patients and patients who do not understand Danish.

The Danish Ministry of Culture's action plan

Most recently the Minister for Culture has tabled a Bill Amending the Act on Museums. The Bill proposes that in order for museums to obtain and keep subsidies they must endeavour to provide the greatest possible accessibility for, among others, persons with disabilities. Accessibility here means not only physical accessibility but also the possibility of sign language interpretation.

Subtitling of television broadcasts

Deaf persons can be informed through the use of subtitling or sign language interpretation in the public service channels' television broadcasts. However, far from all Danish-language broadcasts are subtitled. In the Danish Act on Radio and Television Broadcasting of 2000, it is made clear that the public service channels are under an obligation to ensure that disabled persons' access to public service programmes is strengthened. This is to be done by utilising new technologies, for example, subtitling etc. of Danish-language television programmes.

Films

The aim of the Danish Film Institute under the Ministry of Culture is to obtain a subsidy arrangement for the subtitling of Danish films for the benefit of deaf and hearing-impaired persons. So far one film has been subtitled and two more are on their way. The Institute also grants subsidies to cinemas which wish to install an induction loop system.

The Bible in Danish Sign Language

A video with some of the most important biblical texts interpreted into sign language has been released. To make the translation more accurate it was done directly from Greek and Hebrew into sign language. A special translation committee to accomplish the work consisted of four people: a deaf linguistics student, a deaf teacher of interpreters, a hearing priest and a hearing sign language expert. Together they have worked half a year to translate 26 texts and 8 hymns. There are still many important texts to translate and the committee started on new texts in January 2002 and will continue for another four years. The aim is to translate the whole of the New Testament into sign language and make it available on DVD, CD-rom and on the Internet. So far it is only available on VHS. The project cost for the whole period is estimated to be 1.1 million euros and is sponsored by the Danish Church Ministry and a wide range of funds.

40

3.5. Finland[1]

The Finnish Sign Language is the mother tongue of about 5,000 deaf people. In addition to this, about 10,000 hearing people use it as their second mother tongue, second language or foreign language. The Research Centre on National Languages has studied Finnish Sign Language since 1984. The Act on The Research Centre on National Languages (591/1996) states that the research centre has to take care of Finnish Sign Language research and maintenance. The Finnish Sign Language Board on language was established in 1997. It is submitted to the Research Centre on National Languages and the work conducted has a basis in the Decree on The Research Centre on National Languages (758/1996).

The Sign Language of the Finland-Swedish deaf can be considered a separate language from the main variant of the Finnish Sign Language. The Finland-Swedish Sign Language is the mother tongue of about 200 deaf people. Deaf Finns using Finland-Swedish Sign Language form a small minority that is in danger of extinction. The school for deaf Finns using Swedish Sign Language was closed down in 1993. Most deaf children, young people and adults of working age who use the Finland-Swedish Sign Language have emigrated to Sweden.

A research project on Finland-Swedish Sign Language studied the situation of their language in Finland in the period 1998-2002. The sign language used by them has been recorded on video and analysed. The research project aims to publish a Finland-Swedish Sign Language dictionary.

Legislation

Finland is one of the first countries in the world to have adopted sign language in its constitution (1995). The Constitution Act of Finland (731/1999) was renewed in 1999 and contains the general anti-discrimination clause in section 6. The anti-discrimination clause rules that without acceptable

1. In Finland, the European Charter for Regional or Minority Languages (1992) entered into force on 1 March 1998.

grounds, no one shall be placed in a different position because of, e.g., language and disability. According to the fundamental statement, the anti-discrimination clause covers both direct and indirect discrimination. Besides this, according to section 17, the rights of those who use sign language and of those who require interpretation or translation services because of disability shall be guaranteed by the Act of Parliament.

Interpretation Services

According to the Act on Services and Assistance for the Disabled (380/1987), section 8, the municipality shall provide severely disabled persons with reasonable interpretation services and service accommodation if, because of their disability or illness, their needs to have assistance in order to manage their everyday affairs.

In section 7 of the Degree on Support and Assistance for the Disabled (759/1987) it is stated that interpretation services comprise all interpretation in sign language or other methods for clarifying communication needed for work, studies, social participation, recreation or any other corresponding purpose. According to section 8, in the arrangement of interpretation services, a person shall be considered severely disabled aurally and visually, or if he/she has a severe speech defect. According to section 9, interpretation services shall be arranged so that a severely aurally and visually disabled (deafblind) person has the possibility of receiving at least 240, and any other person referred to in section 8 at least 120, hours of interpretation services during a calendar year.

Education

In section 10 of the law on basic education (628/1998) it is stated that the language used for teaching in a school can be Finnish Sign Language. The guardian can also choose a second language, which is taught as a mother tongue. In the law on upper secondary schools (629/1998) it is ruled that the language used in teaching can be Finnish Sign Language. The student can choose the language in which he/she is taught. If the student so chooses, a sign language can also be taught as a mother tongue. For high school, vocational and university education sign language interpretation services are provided according to the legislation in force.

Broadcasting

According to the Act on Yleisradio Oy (746/1998), section 7, Yleisradio Oy has to treat in its broadcasting Finnish and Swedish-speaking citizens on equal grounds and to produce services in the Saame and Romany languages and in sign language as well as, where applicable, for other language groups in the country. Finnish TV sends daily news in sign language and the Association of the Deaf publishes a monthly video bulletin in sign language.

Training of professionals

A training programme for class teachers of Finnish Sign Language users started in the autumn of 1998, and 10 students began their studies. In autumn 2001 another group commenced studies. University level studies in sign language are popular subjects both at Turku and Jyväskylä Universities. In autumn 1998 a study programme regarding sign languages was started at the University of Jyväskylä.

Sign Language Instructor

The basic diploma in Finnish Sign language instruction started in autumn 2001. The professional title is "Sign Language Instructor" and it consists of 120 credit weeks. It is a completely new profession in Finland.

Finnish Sign Language Interpreters

Training of Finnish Sign Language interpreters moved from a second level college to a polytechnic institute of higher learning. The training consists of 140 credit weeks.

43

Development Activities

Sign Language Teaching

The Finnish Association of the Deaf, obtained financing from the Finnish Slot Machine Association for the HELY Project aimed at relatives of and people working with the deaf. This project runs from 2001-2006. The project studies how languages in general are taught and what methods can be applied to teaching sign languages to hearing people. A teaching unit is being created, based on the level of skills, the examination system is being renewed and new teaching material is being produced.

The National Board of Education ratified the bases for a new curriculum that was implemented at pre-school level for a pilot project from 2000-2001. Account was taken of sign language users as an individual group. The Finnish Association of the Deaf participated in the preparatory process, and they were also asked to make a statement regarding the educational curriculum.

Interpretation Services and Interpreters

The Research and Development Center for Welfare and Health (STAKES) has obtained financing from the Ministry of Social Affairs and Health for the new project. Its objective was to encourage municipalities to arrange the interpretation services for a person considered disabled aurally or with a speech defect. The project ran from 2001-2003.

The Humanities Polytechnic Human Connections (HUMAK) research project aims to improve the working situation of sign language interpreters.

Virtual School Networks

The three-year Virtuopy (Virtual Study Tutor) Project, financed by the European Social Fund (ESF) and the Ministry of Education, began in 2000, and its objective is to create in the data networks virtual study and vocational tutoring for all Finnish Sign Language user groups.

Six comprehensive schools of deaf people and two adult schools participate in the Virtual School Project, initiated in 1999, which is co-ordinated by the Finnish Association of the Deaf. Its objective is to create for Sign Language users of all ages a suitable Open Learning Environment, network pedagogy and a visual user interface for Sign Language users.

TV Programmes

The company ProSign Oy produces multimedia in Finnish Sign Language and was founded in 1998. It has produced, among other things, children's programmes for TV in Finnish Sign Language and the educational programme "I came, I saw, I signed".

Church

At church the needs of those who use sign language have been taken into account so that in 1999, the Church Council (Lutheran) began translating the church manual into sign language. It is planned to make the translation of church texts a permanent activity.

Publications

The Research and Development Centre for Welfare and Health (STAKES) carried out a study on the present status and functionality of Finnish Sign Language interpretation. The report was published, and it stated that there is room for improvement. According to the research, there are shortcomings in the services and their provision, especially the following: inadequate number of sign language interpreters, differences in the availability of services between various groups of disabled people, regional differences and quality questions.

The basic dictionary of Finnish Sign Language was published in 1998. The dictionary was a joint venture of The Finnish Association of the Deaf and The Research Centre on National Languages. The dictionary was nominated for the "Finnish Knowledge" contest, and received much attention.

In autumn 2000, a study called "If All Hearing People Could Use Sign Language" was published with support from the Service Foundation for the Deaf and the Finnish Federation for Social Welfare and Health. It deals with the well-being of Finnish deaf people.

A survey on sign language "The Users of Sign Language in Finland" by The Finnish Association of the Deaf was published in Autumn 2000.

A teaching package in Finnish Sign Language was completed in 2001 by the Finnish Association of the Deaf aimed at schools that teach social and health sciences.

3.6. France[1]

Call for recognition of LSF

At the end of the national "silent" march for the recognition of French Sign Language (LSF) on 17 March 1999, the National Federation of the Deaf in France, supported by 3,000 deaf people, handed a private members bill concerning rights of the deaf, the right to use LSF and a call for recognition of LSF to Mr. Laurent Fabius, former President of the French National Assembly.

The FNSF (*Fédération Nationale des Sourds de France*) promotes the use of LSF as a first language, with written French as a second language for the purposes of written communication. According to the FNSF, LSF should be available and used in everyday communication with deaf people, beginning at nursery school – right through the professional life of deaf people. LSF was the first sign language that received a great deal of attention and recognition because of the work of Charles Michel de l'Epée who, in the 1800s, established the first public school for the deaf in the world. Today, academic research clearly shows that LSF is a complete language with its own grammar, vocabulary, etc.

---

1. France signed the European Charter for Regional or Minority Languages (1992) on 7 May 1999.

Many non-deaf persons wish to learn LSF as a second or foreign language. The FNSF request that LSF be offered as a subject for examination in secondary schools, and as an optional subject for the Baccalauréat examination. There is increased demand for LSF courses, but unfortunately there are not enough qualified teachers available. In April 1999, an action committee was established by three major organisations: IRIS (Toulouse), ALSF (Paris), IVT (Vincennes). This action committee works together to develop a basic training package for teaching LSF. The committee also intends to develop educational methods for teaching LSF. These approaches will then be disseminated across France.

Bilingual education

On 12 October 2000, a representative of the Minister of Education observed the appalling state of education made available to deaf teenagers. The FNSF challenged the Minister's representative to compare what he saw with the bilingual approach to education that is in place at IRIS, Toulouse. According to the FNSF, the representative reported on his visits to the Education Office for the Toulouse Region and called for the region to take whatever measures were necessary to authorise bilingual education. The FNSF is waiting for similar measures to be taken at national level.

Mr. Jean-Pierre SUEUR, Lord Mayor of Orleans, and principal member in charge of the Private Members Bill concerning the recognition of LSF, accepted that the complexity of the education system needed to be examined in more detail.

Mr. Alain SEKSIG, the advisor to the Ministers responsible for National Education, sent a letter to all principal teachers in schools for the deaf encouraging them to promote the use of LSF in teaching in their schools.

Recognition of French Sign Language

On 1 March 2004, the French Senate adopted a draft law on equal rights and equality of opportunity, participation and citizenship of people with disabilities, which includes for the first

47

time a definition of the term " disability " and enshrines the right to compensation. The draft law was subject to more than 150 amendments, of which more than 20 were unanimously adopted, including the one officially recognising sign language.

3.7. Germany[1]

Germany comprises 16 federal states (*"Länder"*), each having an elected parliament and an elected government in its own right. If not stated otherwise by the constitution, the *"Länder"* are independent in their decision-making process. This includes all legal actions concerning educational matters as well as, for example, the recognition of sign language. This means that decisions – also concerning sign language – are situated partly at the Federal level and partly at the level of the *"Länder"*.

Deaf people are engaged in a wide range of political activities. During a festival of deaf culture in Hamburg in 1993, a demonstration was organised, followed by another in Munich in 1995. Round table meetings and discussions with a large number of politicians have been arranged in order to inform them about deafness in general and the importance of sign language for the deaf community. Many of these politicians felt they had to promote deaf people's concerns more than they had previously done so and became engaged in various political activities in this field.

The German Deaf Association saw a change in the education of deaf children. Whereas during the early 1990s, education was exclusively oral with some use of signed German, the end of the decade saw more and more use of German Sign Language and bilingual projects, and students of special education for the deaf are now obliged to take classes in German

1. In Germany, the European Charter for Regional or Minority Languages (1992) entered into force on 1 January 1999.

Sign Language. More and more German Sign Language is used in the classroom.

The recognition of German Sign Language

Since 1989 the German Deaf Association has been fighting for the recognition of German Sign Language.

Above all there was a demand for:

– the training of sign language interpreters and the possibility to study German Sign Language at university;

– clear regulations regarding the payment of German Sign Language interpreters;

– the inclusion of German Sign Language in schools: German Sign Language classes for teachers and the use of German Sign Language in the education of severely hearing-impaired children and young adults;

– German Sign Language interpreters on TV.

From the beginning the German Deaf Association has been strongly supported by German universities, which have begun to carry out research into German Sign Language, especially the Institute for German Sign Language and Communication of the Deaf, University of Hamburg. Like many other linguists abroad, linguists working there recognised that German Sign Language is a true language in its own right. To date the German Deaf Association has achieved:

– the promotion of the recognition of German Sign Language from 1993 to 1996 by the parliaments of Saxony, Sachsen-Anhalt, Thuringia and Hesse in order to achieve nationwide recognition;

– the decision of all 16 Ministers of Labour and all the Ministers of Social Affairs to recognise German Sign Language in 1994;

– the decisions of the Council of Ministers regarding the recognition of Sign Language in 1997, 1998 and 1999;

– the first debate on the recognition of German Sign Language at the national German Parliament in 1998;

– German sign language was put on the agenda by Bündnis 90/Die Grünen (Green Party) and the SPD (Social Democrats) in their common guidelines drawn up after having won the election.

School education

The responsibility of the federal states (*"Länder"*) for education and school also leads to differences in the application of German Sign Language in the education of deaf or hearing-impaired pupils. Therefore each state decides for itself how to use German Sign Language in schools for special educational needs. Related to that is the question of the duty for students of special education of hearing-impaired pupils to learn the German Sign Language. Apart from these differences, there is consensus among the responsible ministers that in cases of severe hearing impairments the use of sign language has to be developed to give the children an adequate way of expression.

Sign Language Interpreting

The Book No. 9 of the Social Code and the Act on Equal Opportunities for Disabled Persons brought clear regulations for the payment of interpreters needed for conversation. Hearing-impaired persons can now get sign language interpretation for their contacts:

– with all funds and administrations of social law including the delivery of social benefits;
– with all public administrations under federal law, and;
– as personal assistance for their work.

Most federal states (*"Länder"*) are following this direction, creating similar laws for their administrations. For other necessary purposes, sign interpretation is paid as social assistance under its conditions which include an income check.

These improvements lead to a higher demand for sign language interpreters, which can not always be met as the number of sign language interpreters is very small. According to a recent survey, most interpreters work part-time and there

50

are only about 50 full-time interpreters available. This means that each deaf person could book an interpreter for an average of two hours a year.

It is, however, a great success to have several universities in Germany (Hamburg, Frankfurt and Magdeburg) offering interpreter training at a high level.

In 1999 the "Bavarian Institute for the Promotion of Communication of the Deaf and the hearing-impaired" was founded to carry out more research into the education and certification of German Sign Language/English interpreters and German Sign Language teachers.

Sign language interpreting on TV

There is still very little German Sign Language visible on TV. Subtitling is offered exclusively by state-run broadcasting stations and is available for only a very narrow range of programmes. The only exception is the private broadcasting station "Pro7", which offers Saturday night programmes with subtitles. The state-run broadcasting station, "Phoenix", does have interpreters on the 8 p.m. news every evening as well as on a news round-up programme, broadcast later at night. These same programmes are broadcast on "ZDF" at the same time without interpreters, so that hearing people cannot complain about the "interference" of sign language/sub-titles. Apart from this there are no regulatory interpreted programmes available so far.

Act on Equal Opportunities for Disabled Persons

With the Act on Equal Opportunities for Disabled Persons, which entered into force on 1 May 2002, the ban on discrimination contained in the Basic Law over and above social law is implemented across the whole public law area. The Act serves to ensure the equal rights of disabled persons in all fields of life and to put them into practice in everyday life. It is a matter of eliminating the obstacles standing in the way of equal opportunities. The core of the Act on Equal Opportunities for Disabled Persons is the creation of comprehensively understood barrier-free environments. Barrier-free environments are conditional on comprehensive access and unrestricted use of all designed environments.

The goal of general barrier-free environments includes the development of barrier-free communication such as using sign language interpreters or barrier-free electronic media. In addition three ordinances entered into force in July 2002 which obliged federal authorities to ensure barrier-free environments in the broadest sense of the word. Hearing- or speech-impaired persons have the right when defending their own rights in administrative procedures with all federal authorities to communicate in German Sign Language with signs supporting spoken language or via other suitable communication aids. The authorities have to meet the costs.

The Act on Equal Opportunities for Disabled Persons recognises German Sign Language as a language in its own right (§6). Here the yearlong efforts of the German Deaf Association for the recognition of German Sign Language have finally paid off. Previously, in July 2001, the Code of Social Law No. IX was adopted, which included, *inter alia,* the right for deaf people to use sign language when communicating with public authorities. The passing of the law is a great achievement in the struggle to break down communication barriers. The German Deaf Association is very pleased with the result, and hopes it will be a strong motivation for the federal states (*"Länder"*) of Germany to further promote the recognition and use of sign language in their regions.

3.8. Ireland[1]

Sign Language

The Deaf Community in Ireland (about 5,000 people) regard Irish Sign Language (ISL) as their first language which differs from signed English. There have been a number of develop-

---

1. Ireland has not signed the European Charter for Regional or Minority Languages (1992).

ments in relation to sign languages both in legislation and policies generally which are summarised below.

The most prominent practical measures to promote ISL have taken place in the education system:

a. recognition in the Education Act (1998) which interprets "support services" to be services provided to students or their parents, schools or centres of education and include "provision for students learning through Irish sign language or other sign language";

b. the provision of in-service training in ISL for all teachers in the special schools for deaf students;

c. the provision/employment of deaf people as Special Needs Assistants (SNAs) in classes in certain schools who act as communication workers and assist the hearing class teachers to mediate parts of the curriculum for the deaf sign-dependent pupils;

d. the Centre for Deaf Studies which was established by the government in November 2001 to focus on training ISL tutors and ISL/English interpreters. This is an important development as there are few professional ISL/English interpreters;

e. the Linkup Literacy Project for which the Irish Deaf Society received funding to improve and sustain English as a second language for deaf persons. The project will develop a curriculum and train tutors who will in turn teach deaf people through ISL;

f. the Home ISL Tuition Scheme which is funded by the government and involves grants to parents of deaf children for the purposes of hiring ISL tutors for their children. The scheme is available to school-going pupils who require this support for 1 or 2 hours per week during school term and for 7.5 hours per week during July and August. The scheme will be reviewed;

g. deaf third level students are supported by sign language interpreters;

53

h. a pilot project pre-school for deaf children has been established and is funded by the Department of Education and Science. An important part of this pre-school is the provision of classes in ISL for 30 parents, siblings and other family members.

Media

National TV channels run a number of news bulletins with a sign language interpreter, but these are mainly signed in English. Under the Broadcasting Act 2001, the Broadcasting Commission of Ireland is currently in the process of developing access rules to enhance the provision of TV and radio services to people with a hearing impairment. This also entails consultation with service providers, interest groups and the Broadcasting Commission.

Irish Sign Link

Irish Sign Link is the national agency of sign language interpreters. It received a grant from the government and receives commission levied from interpreting fees.

3.9. Italy[1]

In Italy, ENS (*Ente Nazionale dei Sordomuti*) was charged with establishing a National Committee for Sign Language as part of the EUD Sign Languages Project. This committee worked intensively from December 1996 to June 1997, presenting bills to Parliament for the recognition of Italian Sign Language in the educational environment, in university environments and in the mass media.

Recognition of Italian Sign Language (LIS)

A total of four bills have been presented to the Italian Parliament regarding the recognition of Italian Sign Language. These include Bill Nos. 4000, 5556, 3083 and 6637.

---

1. Italy signed the European Charter for Regional or Minority Languages (1992) on 27 June 2000.

These bills have not yet been passed, but if they had, they would have guaranteed deaf individuals the freedom to use LIS in all areas of their lives. It is not a matter of pitching oral language versus a signed language: many deaf people are already bilingual to a greater or lesser degree insofar as they know written Italian and LIS. It is more a case of recognising LIS and increasing opportunities for its use in educational, social and work settings, just as was previously recommended by the European Parliament in their 1988 and 1998 resolutions.

Education legislation for school settings

Proposals to include the teaching of LIS to train support teachers have been accepted. For the first time in Italy, a number of hours in LIS training must be completed in order to qualify for the qualification awarded by the Ministry for Public Instruction for support teachers. Communication assistants, deaf and hearing, are now working throughout Italy. Their role is to facilitate communication between deaf students, their classmates and teachers through LIS. Among many European projects that have taken place, one focused on offering training to deaf people to become communication assistants. Besides possessing certain teaching skills, these professionals must be skilled in communication strategies for use with deaf people and have a certain degree of knowledge of LIS (as set down in Law No. 104/92).

An increasing number of families choose a bilingual education for their deaf child (LIS and Italian), and they call on their governments and local agencies (municipal or provincial) to provide classroom assistants in their children's classrooms. At nursery school and elementary school, the assistant is often a deaf person. In addition, the committee's suggestion to place more than one deaf child in each classroom has been implemented by many schools throughout Italy.

The Italian school system has recently been reformed. One reform gives schools more autonomy in deciding on the programme of studies which has led to the establishment of new

55

LIS as a second language courses for hearing students in places like Palermo, Guidonia (Rome), Cossato (Biella), etc. This change opens up many new opportunities for ENS and for LIS.

University

Law 104/92 provides for the presence of LIS interpreters. Law No. 17 of 28/01/1999 guaranteed funding for tutors, though each university may act autonomously. Four years ago, ENS established specialised internal departments where deaf and hearing experts work side by side. These departments include FALiCs (Training and Updating in LIS and Deaf culture) and SEU (School, Education, University). The two departments work in tandem and collaborate when in contact with external organisations and institutions such as the two national associations of interpreters – ANIOS and ANIMU.

Mass media

Italian regulations require that government-owned television stations must offer services to people with disabilities (by virtue of their service contract that is renewable every three years). Such services are also considered to be a just return for taxes that are paid for television licenses. ENS has held sit-in demonstrations and protests, which have resulted in the provision of two national television live news programmes per day with closed captioning and three pre-recorded new bulletins provided with LIS interpretation. In addition, the number of closed-captioned programmes has increased by 20% due to the close collaboration of Televideo and ENS.

3.10. Luxembourg[1]

General comments

The trilingualism practised in Luxembourg is a result of its geographical location between French-speaking and German-

---

1. Luxembourg signed the European Charter for Regional or Minority Languages (1992) on 5 November 1992.

speaking countries. Consequently, there are three official languages in Luxembourg: Luxembourgish (native tongue), German and French.

The use of languages is not governed by the constitution but by a law passed on 24 February 1984. This law, known as the law of 24 February 1984 on language use, complies with the unwritten constitutional law establishing the use of languages in the Grand Duchy of Luxembourg.

For that reason, and given the country's specific geographical situation, hearing pupils receive intensive language training during their schooling. Young hearing Luxembourgers learn Luxembourgish as their native language. In primary schools, German is taught as a first foreign language from the first year onwards. From the second year on, French and German are taught in parallel. In secondary schools, English is the third compulsory foreign language.

Legislation and constitution

Luxembourg has no legislation referring to the use of a sign language. Moreover, the constitution does not currently provide for any fundamental right concerning the use of such a language.

Education of the hearing-impaired

The teaching of deaf and hearing-impaired pupils receiving school education at the Centre de Logopédie is oral, supported by signing, in sign-supported Luxembourgish or German. The only school for deaf and hearing-impaired children in Luxembourg is the Centre de Logopédie, one of whose tasks is to cater for the needs, at an early age, of hearing-impaired children through specialised teaching. However, for more than 100 years the deaf and hearing-impaired were educated solely in spoken German, using the oral approach. At the time the language used to teach deaf and hearing-impaired children was German since spoken German is very close to written German and also to Luxembourgish.

Moreover, children are taught to read and write in German in the Grand Duchy.

1993 saw the introduction of teaching for deaf children with multiple disabilities in sign-supported German, an oral approach where each word is accompanied simultaneously by a sign borrowed from German Sign Language. It is an oral language visualisation system. (In German this visualisation method is called LBG – *Lautsprachbegleitende Gebärden.*) As of the school year 2002/2003 all deaf and hearing-impaired children schools at the *Centre de Logopédie* are taught in sign-supported German or Luxembourgish for early learning and pre-school education and in sign-supported German for primary education. In sign-supported Luxembourgish, German signs are used to ensure a coherent system for the pupils. Following their compulsory schooling in Luxembourg some of them go on to learn German Sign Language in establishments in the neighbouring regions of Germany with a view to post-secondary studies in sign language.

No sign language recognised in Luxembourg is taught at present. A sign language is generally based on the national language of the country concerned. This means that, in Luxembourg, sign language should be based on Luxembourgish, the native language of the Luxembourgers. However, such a Luxembourgish-based sign language does not exist.

Sign language in everyday life

Over the years though, a sign language specific to the country has developed, partly based on German sign language and partly comprising gestures with national connotations. This "Luxembourgish" gestural language is not yet recognised and has no official status.

Sign language and culture

The Luxembourgish Deaf Association (*Verein der Gehörlosen und Schwerhörigen Luxembourg*) has participated twice in the Language Festival in which students of all schools of the

Grand Duchy of Luxembourg take part. The festival provides an opportunity for the Deaf Association to demonstrate sign languages in use, use of finger spelling, sign language-based multi-media, such as CD-ROMs and videos, and sign language sketches for the event. Recently an umbrella organisation has been set up for hearing-impaired and deaf people in Luxembourg. In addition, there is a grouping of young deaf people, "Daaflux", who organise meetings to exchange advice.

Television

The Luxembourg Government has been encouraging "RTL Télé Lëtzebuerg" to make its news services more accessible to the deaf and hearing-impaired through German subtitling during the television news, which is broadcast in Luxembourgish.

Print media

These reflect the multilingual climate in Luxembourg. Despite its small size, Luxembourg has six national daily newspapers. The articles are written in German, French and sometimes in Luxembourgish in four dailies.

Mention of sign languages at ministerial and parliamentary level

The Ministry of the Family, Social Solidarity and Youth, competent for matters relating to people with disabilities, has pointed out that the use of sign language is necessary. The issue of sign languages has recently been raised in a parliamentary question. Furthermore, the parliament has also broached the question of providing sign language interpreters in museums to guide deaf people.

Policy on people with disabilities

In 1995, as part of the governmental reorganisation, the Ministry of the Family, responsible for co-ordinating policy on people with disabilities, drew up an action plan which resulted in the first national colloquy on this topic (1997), to which the Luxembourgish Deaf Association was invited. However, sign languages are not mentioned in this pro-gramme.

Conclusion

The situation in the spheres of education, culture and politics shows that there is a long way to go before sign language is used and recognised widely in Luxembourg. Given its geo-graphical location, Luxembourg could co-operate with the regions bordering on the Grande Région area, comprising Luxembourg, Lorraine (France), Rheinland-Pfalz and Saarland (both Germany) and the province of Luxembourg (Belgium), and participate in sign language projects with a regional focus in the *Grande Région* geared to exchanging best practice.

3.11. The Netherlands[1]

During the past twenty years a fundamental change has taken place within Dutch society as regards the importance of the Dutch Sign Language. This change has influenced the gov-ernment's views regarding the status and the use of the Dutch Sign Language. The Cabinet acknowledges that the Dutch Sign Language is a vital communication element for many people who have a hearing disability. Materially speaking, this should result in an improved social position of those with a hearing disability. The social recognition of a Dutch Sign Language is not under discussion. As such, several measures have been announced per sector. The Cabinet has also announced its opinion that there should be one standard Dutch Sign Language. Standardisation is essential for the implementation process, such as developing a curriculum for schooling, educational tools, activities and products provided by the Dutch Sign Language Centre, training courses for inter-preters for the deaf, etc. As regards a Dutch Sign Language being recognised, this reaction indicates that it will only be

---

1. In the Netherlands, the European Charter for Regional or Minority Languages (1992) entered into force on 1 March 1998.

under discussion when one single Dutch Sign Language (with no variants) has been determined as the standard.

Legal recognition of the Dutch Sign Language

In March 1996, the State Secretary for Education established the Dutch Sign Language Committee. This committee was requested to advise on the importance of the Dutch Sign Language (DSL) and on its use. In 1997 it presented its report entitled "More than just a Gesture". In this report the Dutch Sign Language Committee indicated the importance of recognising the Dutch Sign Language (DSL) for those who use it, namely the deaf and hard of hearing. In its report, the committee reached the conclusion that the government must proceed to a formal recognition of a Dutch Sign Language in order to guarantee that anyone who wishes can use this language and that certain target groups are entitled to relevant provisions and facilities.

The committee believes that recognition of a Dutch Sign Language must actually result in:

- guarantees for learning the Dutch Sign Language;
- guarantees that people who use the Dutch Sign Language are not discriminated against;
- facilities for the use of the Dutch Sign Language in communication between the deaf and the hearing;
- guarantees that the deaf can learn the Dutch language insofar as this lies within their capabilities.

The committee has studied the various possibilities of officially establishing the recognition of a Dutch Sign Language. According to the committee, the following variants exist:

Regularisation in the constitution

Some countries have provided for the national sign language in this manner. When recognised through the constitution, the use of the language concerned can be regulated as a civil right, for instance. However, the position of the Dutch language has hardly been provided for in the Netherlands; the

61

constitution states nothing on it. Only since 1995 has it been laid down in the General Administrative Law Act that administrative bodies must use the Dutch language. It is also only recent that legislation on education declares the language in which schooling is to be provided. The fact that the position of the Dutch language is not provided for in the constitution does not make it any easier to provide for a Dutch sign language. Nor is it easy to make any amendments to the constitution. Opting for this variant implies, therefore, that something must also be regulated with regard to the Dutch language. As this option was not considered for the Dutch language, it is not the right option for the Dutch Sign Language either.

Anti-discrimination legislation

Another option may possibly be anti-discrimination legislation expressly prohibiting discrimination on the basis of a disability. Incidentally, the anti-discrimination bill of 2003 does not concern recognition of provisions that are essential for the people with disabilities, such as sign language, but a general legal regulation for equal treatment of the disabled and protection against unwelcome discrimination. Anti-discrimination legislation can be the legal basis for the right to the use of sign language and interpreters for the deaf and expresses the importance that the legislator attaches to equal rights.

Specific legislation

Another possibility is not to opt for one (statutory) regulation to embed the Dutch Sign Language, but to make separate regulations (or to adapt existing regulations) for sundry components and/or for the use of this language in various social domains instead. The two could also be combined. The individual regulations can relate to the use of the DSL, to learning the DSL and to the right of having an interpreter for the deaf during schooling, in employment situations, legal situations and in private life. Much can thus be regulated and focused on specific situations. A major emancipatory effect can emanate from these specific measures.

Islamic signs added to Dutch Sign Language, prompted by Muslim parents[1]

Dutch Sign Language was recently enriched with 163 signs concerning the Islam religion. Effatha, an institution where deaf children learn sign language (among other things), took the initiative to develop the Islamic signs. The 163 signs – presented on video and CD-ROM – enable children and adults who use Dutch Sign Language to learn and communicate about the Islam religion.

The signs were developed after frequent questions from Muslim parents of deaf children, who were unable to communicate with their children about Islam. The Dutch Sign Language so far contained no signs for typical Islamic words. Deaf Muslim children, who accompany their parents to the mosque, knew the rituals but were unable to learn about the background of the rituals and the contents of the Koran. And just as important, deaf adults and children were unable to talk and discuss Islam with each other. The signs are also important for communication between teachers and students at school, conversation among students, and among adults. For example, around 40% of the deaf children who take lessons at the Effatha institution are Muslims.

Every human being has the right to communicate on whatever subject; language has to enable that. The project team who developed the Islamic signs, considered this basic right as their leading principle and motivation. The signs were mostly imported from Morocco, after an unsuccessful search in the Netherlands and other European countries for useful signs concerning Islamic teachings and rituals. It turns out that the 163 new signs still offer little opportunity for a really profound conversation, but a significant start has been made. In about one and a half years the basic list will be evaluated and Effatha may consider investment in a further extension of the list. The Effatha team does not intend to introduce

---

1. Petra Noordhuis in Trouw, Islam gebarentaal, 30/10/2002. Translated by Agnes van Wijnen on www.disabilityworld.com

Christian, Hindu or Buddhist signs in the near future. There seem to be enough Christian signs in the Dutch Sign Language. Compared to the high costs with which such a project is confronted, there is so far not enough demand for Hindu or Buddhist signs in the Netherlands. The basic list of Islamic signs will also shortly be available in print.

3.12. Norway[1]

Norway has become accustomed to the idea of bilingualism. The population consists of 4.3 million people having two written standards to contend with, and a native population of Sami who have their own language, schools and curricula. Most Norwegians speak at least one foreign language. Recent reforms in the education system have led to the introduction of bilingual education for deaf children.

Norwegian Sign Language and the constitution

The Norwegian Association of the Deaf (NAD) made a proposal to the relevant ministry to establish a Sign Language Act in 1990. The NAD wanted Norwegian Sign Language to be recognised as the first language and stressed among others the importance of a syllabus in Norwegian Sign Language as first language. As a result, the Education Act makes reference to Norwegian Sign Language as deaf people's first language.

Norwegian Sign Language in the Education Act

In 1997 the right of deaf children to access education in Norwegian Sign Language was stated, in the form of the ministry's provision to the Primary Education Act. In 1998, a new Education Act, covering both primary education (10 years) and secondary education (3 years) and certain aspects of pre-school education (up to age 6 years), was passed in the Norwegian Parliament.

---

1. In Norway, the European Charter for Regional or Minority Languages (1992) entered into force on 1 March 1998.

The new Act states, *inter alia,* the following: Education Act, §§ 2-6: "Pupils having Norwegian Sign Language as their first language have the right to primary education in Norwegian Sign Language and to the subject Norwegian Sign Language as a first language. Instruction in Sign Language is to be given according to the National Curriculum passed by the government. Pre-school children with special requirements for Norwegian Sign Language have the right to such education." The municipality may decide that tuition through the medium of sign language and in the use of sign language shall be provided at a different location than the pupil's local school. Children under compulsory school age, who have a special need for sign language tuition, have the right to such tuition. The ministry issues further regulations. Before a municipality makes any decision pursuant to the first and third paragraph, an expert assessment shall be made.

On 17 September 1999, the parliament passed certain changes to the act. Of special interest is the addition of a statement concerning secondary education: Education Act, §§ 3-9: "Youngsters entitled to secondary education and who have Norwegian Sign Language as their first language, or who are, according to an expert judgement, in need of such education, have the right to choose secondary education in Norwegian Sign Language and in the subject Norwegian Sign Language as first language in a signing environment, or the right to choose to use an interpreter in regular secondary schools. The same applies to adults who are admitted to secondary education. A signing environment represents the schools that offer suitable education done in Norwegian Sign Language and in the subject Norwegian Sign Language as first language for hearing-impaired pupils. The right to education done in Norwegian Sign Language and in the subject Norwegian Sign Language as first language is limited to the courses offered by these schools. Parts of this education can be offered by using an interpreter." The Ministry may issue further regulations, including those concerning admissions.

The legislation secures the *right* of every deaf pre-school child, and every deaf child in primary or secondary school, to

65

receive their education through Norwegian Sign Language if that is their first language, irrespective of whether they attend a school for the deaf, partially hearing units or are main-streamed. Nobody can force a family to choose education in Norwegian Sign Language for their child. The National Curricula, which are passed by the government and are com-pulsory for all children state that the intended outcome for deaf children is functional bilingualism.

Norwegian Sign Language as a subject at university

Norwegian Sign Language is a subject at university for both deaf and hearing people who have NSL as their first language and for people who do not have NSL as their first language.

Teacher qualifications in Norwegian Sign Language

All teachers of the deaf whether they teach at a school for the deaf or at a local school with only one deaf pupil, need knowl-edge and skills in Norwegian Sign Language. The Ministry of Education ran a project in 1996-1997 where 250 teachers of the deaf were offered a full term course in Norwegian Sign Language at the university and at the Teachers Training College with all expenses paid by the government. Now teachers (among others) can attend a one-year full-time course in Norwegian Sign Language (but it is not free of charge). The Ministry of Education states that the minimum qualification in Norwegian Sign Language for teachers is the one-term course.

Norwegian Sign Language courses for parents

Since 1996, parents have been offered 40 weeks of sign lan-guage courses with all expenses paid. These classes are on offer from the moment their child's deafness is discovered until the child is 16 years old.

Sign Language Dictionary

In 1998 the Ministry of Education started a Norwegian Sign Language Dictionary Project.

3.13. Portugal[1]

Education

The Constitution of the Portuguese Republic ensures the entitlement of each individual to free and compulsory education. It is also ensured in the constitution the entitlement both to special education, protection and valuation of the Portuguese Sign Language as a cultural expression and access instrument to education and to equality of opportunities (Article 74, section g and h).

To that end, the National Department for Education and Innovation has defined the conditions regarding the creation, operation and functioning of school units for deaf children and youngsters who are attending public primary and secondary schools (Official Bulletin, series II, no. 104, 1998.06.05, p. 6094).

Official recognition of the interpreters' statute on sign language

For a long time in the past the profession of sign language interpretor was not officially recognised. The profession/occupation as interpreter of Portuguese Sign Language is already included in the National Classification of Professions, but it is only now in a study phase with a view to its regulation.

Access of deaf people to public services

– With regard to the access of deaf people to the Justice System, the Ministry of Justice, the National Secretariat for the Rehabilitation and Integration of People with Disabilities and the Portuguese Federation of Associations for the Deaf have signed an agreement which enables each deaf person who has been asked to go to court or has the need to address any service within the justice system to be assisted and backed up by a Portuguese Sign Language interpreter.

---

1. Portugal has not signed the European Charter for Regional or Minority Languages (1992).

– Agreements have been equally signed among several municipalities, such as those from Lisbon and Cascais and the Association of Interpreters on Portuguese Sign Language with a view to facilitating the access of deaf people to those services.

– Since 1999, there has been an agreement between the National Secretariat for the Rehabilitation and Integration of People with Disabilities and that same Association of Interpreters on Portuguese Sign Language with a view to facilitating the access of deaf people to information available within the framework of meetings, conferences, seminars and other events promoted by this Secretariat, by means of an interpretation service on sign language.

Access of deaf people to television broadcasting

Act 31-A/98 of 14 July 1998, changed by the Act 8/2002 of 11 February 2002, states that the government must ensure that the broadcasting of the public television stations may be followed by deaf persons or by those with hearing disabilities.

Within this scope, one has witnessed an effort exerted by the four private and public television channels existing in Portugal, so that the majority of the television programmes in Portuguese are followed up by a sign language interpretation service or by a caption service on the screen through the teletext system.

3.14. Slovenia[1]

There are about 6,000 deaf and partially deaf individuals in the Republic of Slovenia, for whom communication is either difficult or impossible. They include 2,500 deaf persons, who mainly use the Slovenian sign language.

The many years of efforts of the deaf and the professional public who are in any way active in promoting the rights of

1. In Slovenia the European Charter for Regional or Minority Languages (1992) entered into force on 1 January 2001.

the deaf have resulted in the legal regulation of the status of the Slovenian Sign Language by relevant state institutions.

The Constitution of the Republic of Slovenia regulates human rights and fundamental freedoms and ensures equality before the law, thus, together with the Declaration of the Rights of Disabled Persons, providing the fundamental legal basis for the preparation of the Sign Language Act.

The aforementioned Act gives deaf citizens the right to use their language, i.e. the Slovenian Sign Language, and the right to be informed by means of techniques adapted to them. In addition, the statute ensures deaf citizens the right to a sign language interpreter when dealing with the authorities, and an additional 30 hours of interpretation for situations at their discretion, and a total of 100 hours of interpretation per year for educational reasons for those with the status of pupil or student.

The Act stipulates that a professional Council for the Slovenian Sign Language shall be established. Its primary task will be to form a global linguistic policy for the Slovenian Sign Language, with the active involvement of the deaf public.

Until now the use of the sign language in the school system has not been obligatory. With the introduction of a nine-year system in primary school education and a modified curriculum, the use of the sign language in the school system will become compulsory. The Centre for Rehabilitation of the Deaf in Ljubljana and the National Union of the Deaf and Partially Deaf of Slovenia are placing great emphasis on the importance of learning the sign language.

Since 1984, the training of sign language interpreters in Slovenia has been carried out by the Association of Interpreters of the Sign Language. There are 43 interpreters in this association and 23 are active.

In Slovenia, similar to other European countries, there has been resistance to increased interest in cochlear implant (CI) operations within the deaf community (in Slovenia there have been 68 such operations). A consensus is gradually emerging among parents, schools for the deaf, the deaf community, and teachers of the deaf in relation to teaching sign language as a form of bilingual education of the deaf.

3.15. Spain[1]

The main activities promoted or carried out by the Ministry of Labour and Social Affairs (Social and Family Affairs and Disabilities Department) to foster the social integration of deaf persons are as follows:

1. support for sign language;
2. telephone relay centres for deaf people;
3. film and television sub-titles;
4. access to information services via the Internet;
5. Act No. 51/2003 of 2 December 2003 on equal opportunities, non-discrimination

Support for sign language

The public authorities have noted that deaf people champion sign language as "their own natural language" and that they have consistently demanded in recent years that it be recognised and that the authorities support its use and dissemination.

A number of activities have been carried out for this purpose, including the project provided for in the parliamentary initiative approved on 16 December 1997 by the Social Policy Committee of the National Assembly and, in particular, that provided for by the motion approved by the full Senate on 13 April 1999, which invites the government to continue and step up "its work to promote sign language as the main language of the deaf community", and requests that a report be submitted on the needs that would arise if this language were recognised.

---

1. In Spain the European Charter for Regional or Minority Languages (1992) entered into force on 1 August 2001.

In this connection, and in the context of its work overseeing labour and social services, the Ministry of Labour and Social Affairs asked its Family Affairs and Disabilities Department to prepare a report, which was published in the Parliament's Official Gazette (Senate, Series I, No. 806, 20 December 1999). The report proposes measures which the authorities might consider when seeking to satisfy the demands of the deaf community. Among these are measures designed "to support interpretation into sign language through partnership agreements with the organisations that are the most representative of deaf persons with a view to covering sign language interpretation needs in future years".

On 21 March 2002, to ensure that the undertakings given by the Ministry of Labour and Social Affairs in the light of this report are fully honoured on a lasting basis, a partnership agreement was negotiated with the Spanish National Federation of Deaf People (CNSE) with the aim of making it easier for deaf persons to be assisted by a sign language interpreter if they wish to communicate with the authorities in this way. The CNSE will play an active part in implementing this agreement and taking it a step further, by making it easier to be assisted by an interpreter when required. The agreement was renewed in 2003 and 2004. In 2002, 2003 and 2004, there was an average of 18,000 cases a year in which sign language interpreting was used, costing a total of 688,625 euros a year, 428,140 euros of which were covered by the Ministry of Labour and Social Affairs.

A telephone relay centre for deaf people

Aim

The main aim of the relay centre is to improve communication between supposedly incompatible text phones and between text and voice telephones. Relays are provided by operators, who pass on the spoken and typed parts of a conversation by typing them out for deaf text phone users and reading them out for hearing voice telephone users. The relay centre provides nationwide cover, 24 hours a day, 365 days a year and is located in Madrid.

Functional features

Network

The relay centre satisfies the main conditions for the standardisation of telephone communications. It has communications protocols based on text phone and mobile phone technology.

Data communication by text phone and mobile phone

The relay centre has integrated devices capable of answering calls in the form of signals from various sources and handling calls from users of text phones with differing communication formats. This makes it possible to process incoming communications from text phones or mobile telephones using one and the same terminal.

Coverage

In addition to its national service, the relay centre handles relay calls to and from foreign countries, conducted in English.

Operating methods

Arrangements for access to the relay centre are as follows:

- Hearing-impaired users first find the telephone number of the relay centre on their visual terminal. Voice telephone users wishing to call a text phone may also make the initial call.

- The interpreter or operator receives the call on his or her terminal and immediately establishes a connection with the hearing person or the deaf person for whom the call is destined, after which the conversation can continue through an interpreter if necessary.

Terminals

The relay centre uses the following facilities:

a. *Text phones*

EDT and Minitel terminals are used in Spain. There are over 10,000 text phones in Spain using the landline telephone network. Mobile phones with text messaging functions are becoming an increasingly widespread means of communication among deaf people. Deaf people like using them because they are practical.

b.   *Fax*

The relay centre can relay messages received by fax. Faxes do not offer the same kind of rapid response as text phones, but deaf people frequently use them because fax machines are easier to operate.

c.   *Videoconferencing*

Although it is not yet in general use, videoconferencing is being used experimentally as a means of communication for deaf people and it is currently being installed at the relay centre.

Staff

The relay centre is reliant on human resources in the form of the operators providing the direct service to the users. The operators are highly experienced in communication with deaf people and have a good knowledge of Spanish Sign Language, which is the basic tool for anyone acting as an intermediary during communications using videoconferencing.

Funding

The Ministry of Labour and Social Affairs covers the centre's operating costs, which amount to over 600,000 euros a year. Users pay for incoming calls to the centre and, under the partnership agreement negotiated by the ministry with the telephone operator, Telefónica, calls are charged at local rates, irrespective of where they come from.

Number of calls

On average the relay centre handles about 20,000 calls per month.

Film and television sub-titles

The Ministry of Labour and Social Affairs promotes and supports the subtitling of television programmes. Measures taken include national and international one-day events to promote sub-titles and active involvement, through the state-run centre for personal autonomy, CEAPAT, in the preparation of a technical subtitling standard by the Spanish industrial standards authority's Committee No. 153 on technical aids.

Access to information services through the Internet

The Ministry of Labour and Social Affairs is negotiating an agreement with the Ministry of Public Administration, through which it will contribute to a project designed to facilitate access to the Internet in order to provide a better public information service. The first step is to adapt the public portal in order to provide the best possible access conditions.

Act No. 51/2003 of 2 December 2003 on equal opportunities, non-discrimination and universal access for persons with disabilities (LIONDAU)

On 3 December 2003, Act No. 51/2003 of 2 December 2003 on equal opportunities, non-discrimination and universal access for persons with disabilities, as passed by the Spanish Parliament, was published in the Spanish Official Gazette.

Section 12 of the final chapter provides as follows in its paragraph on sign language:

"Within two years of the entry into force of this Act, the government shall make arrangements in keeping with the development of Spanish Sign Language, with a view to ensuring that it is possible for deaf and hard-of-hearing persons to learn, master and use it and guaranteeing them freedom of choice when it comes to communicating. This regulation shall be progressively applied in the various areas referred to in section 3 of this Act".

To this end, the government has begun work on regulations on Spanish Sign Language, to ensure that deaf people have access to public services, information, education, the legal system and means of communication.

3.16. Sweden[1]

National Plan of Action for a Disability Policy

In spring 2000, the Swedish Government presented a national disability policy action plan that includes goals with respect to accessibility. Examples of the priorities laid down for the coming years include:

– ensuring that a disability perspective permeates all sectors of society;

– creating an accessible society.

Some of the practical applications of these goals include:

– establishing a national programme to develop the competency of elected representatives, and all persons whose work brings them in contact with people with disabilities;

– resources have been earmarked for increasing disabled people's access to cultural events;

– representatives of disability organisations to form a consultative committee.

When this plan of action was announced in parliament, many deaf representatives were attending the session. Access was provided via sign language interpretation: for the first time, Swedish Sign Language interpreters occupied a central place in parliament.

Education

Deaf and hard-of-hearing children with sign language as their first language are taught at one of the five regional state-run special schools. There is also one national special school for deaf and hearing-impaired pupils who also have a severe learning disability. The emphasis on teaching in sign lan-

---

1. In Sweden, the European Charter for Regional or Minority Languages (1992) entered into force on 1 June 2000.

guage, and thus the need for contact with other deaf children with the same method of communication, has meant that the special school has been retained. The special schools are organised in the National Agency for Special Schools. The agency has the responsibility to develop the special schools and to guarantee a good educational quality in them.

In 1999, the Swedish Parliament agreed that a Swedish Sign Language environment is necessary for pupils who, because of deafness or impaired hearing, cannot attend a comprehensive school. That is, it accepted the principle that education should be provided via Swedish Sign Language. Indeed, the Education Act (1998; 1100, amendment November 1999) says that the goals to be attained by schools with respect to school-leavers who are deaf or hearing-impaired include:

– bilingualism: i.e. ability to use Swedish Sign Language, read Swedish and to express thoughts in Swedish Sign Language as well as through written Swedish;

– ability to communicate in writing in English.

Teacher training

Training for teachers of the deaf is offered alongside the training programme for teachers who will teach in comprehensive schools. Candidates wishing to become teachers of the deaf must demonstrate knowledge of Swedish Sign Language. For several years, the Swedish Association for the Deaf (SDR) has maintained that not all teachers for the deaf need to be trained as special education teachers, although these are also needed in schools for the deaf. Special attention has been paid to the need for teachers of the deaf with the skills to teach the curriculum for schools of the disabled to deaf children who have slight learning disabilities.

Ratification of the Council of Europe's Charter for Regional or Minority Languages in Sweden

As part of the process to ratify the Council of Europe's Charter for Regional or Minority Languages, the Swedish Government decided not to include Swedish Sign Language as a minority language for the purpose of ratification (spring 1999). The SDR has argued the issue in a parliamentary debate and written to all Members of Parliament. All parties expressed their support for Swedish Sign Language though they felt that it could not be encompassed into the Swedish response to the Charter for Regional or Minority Languages.

Anniversary

2001 marked the 20th anniversary of official recognition of Swedish Sign Language in Sweden. In May 1981, the Swedish Parliament decided that: "deaf have to be bilingual to function amongst themselves and in society. Bilingualism on their part means that they have to be fluent in their visual/gestural language and in the language that surrounds them, Swedish." This decision is recognised as acceptance that Swedish Sign Language is the first language of Swedish deaf people.

Swedish Sign Language and parents

In 1997, the Swedish Parliament voted that parents of deaf children and children with impaired hearing should have the right to learn Swedish Sign Language. The state provides for a total of 240 hours of Swedish Sign Language tuition over a period of four years for parents. This training is offered free of charge to parents who also receive compensation for loss of income from employment. The National Agency for Education has developed a curriculum for this programme (SKOLFS 1998:7).

Swedish Sign Language and siblings of deaf children/children of deaf adults

In Sweden it is possible to have Swedish Sign Language as first language education provided a minimum of five pupils are involved (Comprehensive Schools Act SFS 1997:599). This has happened, though not very frequently. The state also provides for weekly courses, most of which are delivered at schools for the deaf. This provides an opportunity for students who have deaf siblings or deaf parents to learn more Swedish

Sign Language and to interact and share experiences amongst themselves.

Swedish Sign Language at comprehensive school and upper secondary school

Since 1995, non-deaf students have had the opportunity to choose Swedish Sign Language as their third language at comprehensive school and at upper secondary school. The curriculum was last changed in 2000 with more hours being added to the programme of study, and more advanced level courses being made available. In the south of Sweden, in Vänersborg, there is an upper secondary school for non-deaf students, which offers the Swedish Sign Language option. As a result, students are taking Swedish Sign Language classes that are as advanced as introductory courses for interpreting students. Indeed, several graduates of the school have been offered places to train as interpreters.

Swedish Sign Language teachers

A one-year programme is available to deaf and hearing students to train as teachers of Swedish Sign Language. This is the only training programme in Sweden for Swedish Sign Language teachers. There are many opportunities for graduates of this programme, as there is a growing demand for Swedish Sign Language teaching in interpreter training programmes, at schools for the deaf (all levels), and in offering Swedish Sign Language classes to parents of deaf children, siblings of deaf children and to children of deaf parents. The Swedish Parliament decided to upgrade the training available for Swedish Sign Language tutors to college-level qualification following pressure from the SDR and those involved in delivering training at Västanvik (autumn 2000).

Information in Swedish Sign Language at the parliament website

"Samhällsguiden" (The Civic Guide) is a manual for all citizens who want to know more about their rights, obligations, the legal system and regulations. The SDR felt that this would be a good place to begin translating materials into Swedish Sign Language. It is now used as part of the course literature for civics at the special schools for the deaf. In February 2000, the Swedish Parliament notified the media that sample elements from the Civic Guide were available on the web in Swedish Sign Language. The media highlighted the launch of the web-site, and after the first week, evaluations showed very positive feedback from Swedish deaf people who had visited the site. (www.samhallsguiden.riksdagen.se)

In connection with the fact that Sweden held the Presidency of the European Union for the first half of 2001, the information unit of the Swedish Parliament has worked in conjunction with the SDR to translate two important chapters of the Civic Guide into Swedish Sign Language. These chapters are: "How Sweden is governed", and a chapter about democracy: "Participate and Influence".

These chapters are available at the parliament's home page. The aim of these translations is to demonstrate the way in which the Swedish civic system functions to sign language users who know Swedish Sign Language.

"Straight Talking Group"

The Swedish Government has a committee whose task is to make information about the Swedish authorities accessible in plain language. They encourage authorities to start projects that encourage clear use of language and every year they award a prize, "The Straight Talking Crystal" to an authority who has been successful in making their information accessible. The theme for the year 2000 was "Straight Talking for People with Disabilities". The SDR and the Parliament's Information Unit were invited to participate in the award ceremony on 19 May 2000, and were invited to speak on the topic "This is how we created the Civic Guide in Sign Language".

Cultural activities

The public libraries provide sign language video programmes for the deaf, with cultural and news programmes, and

79

Swedish Television broadcasts news in sign language daily. In the guidelines decided by the parliament and government, the Swedish public service broadcasting companies (radio, television and educational programmes) have far-reaching demands on their efforts to make programmes accessible to people with disabilities. One of the most important demands is that the number of subtitled programmes shall increase considerably.

The Bible in Swedish Sign Language

On 29 November 2001, 600 deaf people from all over Sweden attended a celebration church service where Queen Silvia received the first edition of the Bible in Swedish Sign Language. The whole of the Marcus Evangelism and five different biblical texts related to the most important religious days during the year, i.e. Christmas and Easter, have been translated. The project, among others, was financed by the Swedish Culture Department, the Swedish Church, the Swedish Bible Company, the Swedish Deaf Association and the Swedish Institute for Disability issues in school.

Health and Medical Service Act (1982)

The Health and Medical Service Act (1982) was amended and the Swedish County Councils are now obliged to provide sign language interpretation to deaf, deafened, deaf-blind and hearing-impaired persons for "everyday interpreting". This means providing interpretation in the working life of the deaf person, in in-service training environments and in leisure and club activities. County councils are subsidised by the state.

Swedish Sign Language interpreters

In autumn 1999, the SDR had a question introduced in the Swedish Parliament regarding the authorisation of Swedish Sign Language interpreters. During the autumn of 2000, the parliament requested that the Swedish National Judicial Board for Public Lands and Funds focus on this issue. Since 1994, the county councils have had responsibility for offering interpreter services. State subsidies allow for expansion of these services. The number of interpreters has subsequently increased, and there are now seven institutes offering Swedish Sign Language/Swedish interpreter training in Sweden. The Swedish National Board of Health and Welfare is responsible for monitoring this issue.

One might expect that because there are more Swedish Sign Language interpreters available that access has increased: however, as more interpreters have become available, demand for interpreter services has increased. Despite that, funding has not increased. This has led to concerns that the county councils will not be able to find the funding to employ the current student interpreters when they graduate from training.

In May 2003, the Swedish Government decided on a public authorisation of Swedish Sign Language interpreters. The Swedish National Board is responsible for the implementation.

3.17. Switzerland[1]

The status of sign languages was raised in the Swiss Parliament in 1994, when the Committee on education, science and culture issued a formal proposal on sign language inviting the Federal Council (government) to recognise it for the purpose of integrating the deaf and hard of hearing and encourage it alongside the spoken language in education, training, research and communication.

The Federal Council accepted the proposal. It is not intended to give sign languages official language status in Switzerland but to grant them a greater role in integration policies and above all to establish legal provisions to encourage their use. Following acceptance of the proposal, sign languages are taken into consideration when new laws are drafted or existing ones revised.

---

1. In Switzerland, the European Charter for Regional or Minority Languages (1992) entered into force on 1 April 1998.

For example, the Federal Invalidity Insurance Act of 19 June 1959 has been amended to take greater account of the needs of persons using sign languages. Currently, such insurance covers the cost of teaching sign language to disabled persons, their families and specialist interpreters. However under the revision of the Act that came into force on 1 January 2004, the permanent dependence allowance has been doubled, which among other things will enable disabled persons to pay for the services of a sign language interpreter.

In addition, on 13 December 2002, parliament passed federal legislation, which came into force on 1 January 2004, to eliminate inequalities affecting disabled persons. The new act seeks to ensure that the needs of all members of the community are taken into account in every aspect of social life. In particular, the first paragraph of Section 14 of the Act requires the authorities to take particular account of the needs of persons with speech, hearing or sight impairments in their dealings with citizens. The third paragraph provides for support for cantonal measures to encourage the use of sign languages in disabled persons' education and vocational training and for national non-profit making organisations and institutions concerned with disabled persons' problems of language and comprehension.

The Act also has special provisions concerning cantons, which in particular must ensure that children and young persons with sight or speech difficulties and their families are able to learn communication techniques adapted to these difficulties.

3.18. United Kingdom[1]

Recognition of British Sign Language in Great Britain

The government recognised British Sign Language (BSL) as a language in its own right in a position statement made to the House of Commons on 18 March 2003.

---

1. In the United Kingdom, the European Charter for Regional or Minority Languages (1992) entered into force on 1 July 2001.

The Disability Discrimination Act (DDA) improves access to BSL by its duty of reasonable adjustment. This requires employers and service providers to consider changes so that employment and goods and services are accessible to disabled people including deaf BSL users.

Government position statement on British Sign Language (BSL)

The government recognises that British Sign Language (BSL) is a language in its own right regularly used by a significant number of people. For an estimated 70,000 deaf people it is their preferred language for participation in everyday life. BSL is a visual-gestural language with its own vocabulary, grammar and syntax.

The government understands that people who use BSL want their language to be protected and promoted in the same way that some minority languages are protected and promoted by the Council of Europe's Charter for Regional or Minority Languages. The Council of Europe is considering how that might be achieved for indigenous sign languages. The government will give careful consideration to any proposals which the Council of Europe might make.

The government has already taken action to improve access to BSL, for example by identifying situations where it might be reasonable for employers and service providers to engage the services of a BSL/English interpreter.

The government will be funding a discrete programme of initiatives to support this statement.

Action following the statement

The Secretary of State for Work and Pensions made a commitment to consult deaf BSL users when deciding priorities for allocating the additional funding. To assist this process a BSL Working Group comprising representatives of organisations of and for deaf people and from key government departments was established. The Working group's first task was to advise government on the priorities described. Following

83

receipt of the group's advice, the Department for Work and Pensions commissioned bids for work in two discrete priority areas. These are bids for work which would either:

– contribute to establishing a GB-wide framework to support the recruitment, training and deployment of BSL tutors, which will enhance their numbers, status and levels of qual- ification,

or which would:

– promote access for BSL users through awareness-raising amongst employers, amongst service providers and in the wider community.

After an open tender exercise, 10 contacts to the value of £1.5m were awarded. The contracts will run until the end of June 2005. Completed projects are expected to leave a long- term impact beyond the end of the project period.

The Working Group will be doing some longer-term strategic thinking and will be advising government in due course on policies and initiatives which would, over time, further increase access for deaf people who use BSL.

Recognition of British and Irish Sign Languages in Northern Ireland

The Secretary of State for Northern Ireland announced recog- nition of British and Irish Sign Languages on 29 March 2004 noting that this followed a statement made by the Secretary of State for Work and Pensions who had announced similar recognition for British Sign Language in Great Britain.

He noted that the 11 Northern Ireland Government Departments would join forces to work proactively in partner- ship with representatives of the deaf community to develop ideas for improving access to public services.

CHAPTER 4 – THE STATUS OF SIGN LANGUAGES IN OBSERVER STATES TO THE PARTIAL AGREEMENT IN THE SOCIAL AND PUBLIC HEALTH FIELD

4.1. Czech Republic[1]

The population of the Czech Republic is approximately 10 million people. It is estimated that of this number about 7,500 – 10,000 are pre-lingually deaf people. This data was obtained by applying the internationally acknowledged coefficient of the number of deaf people to the total population in the relevant state. During the last census in the Czech Republic, which was conducted in 2001, questions on possible disabilities among members of the population were not included. Thus, we must still rely mainly on estimates in this field.

Czech Sign Language and research

In the Czech Republic, deaf people use their own variant of sign language, known as Czech Sign Language. Sign language research is a very young discipline in the Czech context. The most influential body in developing such research is the Institute of Czech Language and Communication Theory at the Faculty of Philosophy, Charles University in Prague. The results of its research are used both in developing the methodology of teaching Czech Sign Language for deaf people and in teaching in the framework of a relatively new study discipline called "Czech in Communication of Deaf People" at the Faculty of Philosophy, Charles University.

Sign Language Act

In 1998, the Parliament of the Czech Republic adopted the Sign Language Act, which recognises the right of deaf people

---

1. The Czech Republic signed the European Charter for Regional or Minority Languages (1992) on 9 November 2000.

to education and communication by means of sign language. For the purpose of the Act, sign language means both Czech Sign Language and signed Czech.

Media laws

The term Media Laws incorporates two acts regulating, *inter alia*, television broadcasting. These are: the Czech Television Act (Czech Television is the only public broadcasting service television in the Czech Republic), which, *inter alia*, stipulates Czech television's obligation to arrange for "at least 70% of all broadcasted programmes to have hidden or displayed sub-titles for people with a hearing impairment or simultaneous interpreting into sign language" and the Act on Radio and Television Broadcasting, which stipulates the obligation for the operators of nationwide television broadcasting to arrange for "at least 15 % of broadcasted programmes to have hidden or displayed sub-titles for people with a hearing impairment".

Television programmes with sign language

Deaf people who use sign language have their own programme on Czech television. It is called "Television Club for Deaf People". It lasts 30 minutes and is broadcast once a month. Another programme on Czech television that is directed primarily at deaf users of sign language is "News in Sign Language", which is broadcast from Monday to Thursday five minutes before the main news programme on Czech television. The programme is presented by deaf news-readers.

Education of deaf people

There are no special schools for deaf people in the Czech Republic. Instead such schools are referred to as "schools for children with a hearing impairment". This generally means that pupils or students with various levels of hearing problems attend classes of these schools together. In the past, the oral method of teaching was used in such schools, and today there is still a lack of teachers who have mastered sign language and understand their pupils or students. Some schools use interpreters who are specialised in education, while other schools engage deaf assistants to help them with teaching.

Until recently, university education was practically unattainable for deaf people. The reasons were the educational level at middle schools for deaf pupils and the impossibility of completing university studies with a good sign language interpreter. In recent years, however, the situation has improved markedly. Deaf people are now able to attend two universities that offer disciplines that are also tailored to the demands of deaf students. These are: Educational drama for deaf students at the Janáāek Academy of Musical Arts in Brno and Czech in Communication of Deaf People at the Faculty of Philosophy of Charles University in Prague.

Sign language courses to the public

Courses of Czech Sign Language or signed Czech are offered by a number of organisations of deaf people and several organisations of interpreters for deaf people. The courses vary in their content and quality. The providers are:

- The Czech Chamber of Sign Language Interpreters
- The Czech Society of Sign Language Interpreters
- The Czech Union of the Deaf
- The Czech-Moravian Union of the Deaf
- The Union of the Deaf and Hard of Hearing in the Czech Republic
- PEVNOST – the Czech Sign Language Centre

Interpretation services and interpreters

ASNEP – The Association of Organisations of the Deaf, Hard of Hearing and their Friends – established "the Centre for Arranging Interpretation Services for Deaf People", which began operations at the end of September 2003. The Centre started to create a database of the Czech Sign Language interpreters as well as a database of signed Czech and articulation interpreters. The data will be updated on a regular basis.

Clients may contact the Centre by telephone, fax, SMS, e-mail or through the form placed on the web.

4.2. Estonia[1]

Estonian Sign Language (ESL) and deaf education

There has been a bilingual teaching approach (bilingual curriculum and deaf teachers) at Tallinn School for the Deaf since 1994, starting from pre-school, and continuing to high-school level. The cornerstone for bilingual teaching was put in place thanks to financial aid from Sweden (SDR, Manillaskolan, Birgittaskolan and other institutions) and thanks to the initiative of a parents' association. This includes:

- basic teaching in ESL for the staff of Tallinn School for the Deaf and parents of deaf children;
- developing materials and methods for teaching ESL;

  Both courses and materials have been developed and managed by the Centre of ESL as from September 2000. This work was previously carried out by the Tallinn School for the Deaf and the Parents Association;

- ESL short courses for students at Tartu University since 1995;
- Interpreter educational training is carried out by the Union of Sign Language Interpreters in the form of short-term projects and is dependent on different funding sources. During 1996-1998 financial aid was received from Finland.

ESL interpretation

"Interpretation" (transliteration) is still carried out into signed exact Estonian. There are approximately 30 interpreters in Estonia, most of whom are free-lance interpreters. There is a lack of educated (Bachelor BA, Masters MA) sign language interpreters available for deaf students at universities. Interpretation service amounts to 36 hours per deaf person

---

1. Estonia has not signed the European Charter for Regional or Minority Languages (1992).

per year. This is free of charge to the deaf person and is offered and guided by the Sign Language Interpreters Union. Finance comes from local governments. Interpretation service for studies at universities and vocational schools is covered by special funding sources.

ESL Research

There is a publication that offers a short description of ESL. This research was carried out by a young researcher working for an MA degree at the Estonian Institute of Humanities. She compared grammatical categories of ESL and Estonian, the spoken majority language of Estonia.

A Commission of standardisation is currently working to compile different Estonian signs. The team consists of interpreters and deaf people and works under the guidance of the Estonian Association for the Deaf. In this project, ESL is recorded on videotape and analysed at the ESL Centre by the Tallinn School for the Deaf.

ESL and television

The Estonian broadcasting authorities offer a daily news programme translation into signed Estonian. Teletext news is available and widely used. For example, the Parents Association spreads information mostly through teletext. There are no special programmes for the deaf.

ESL dictionaries

As research of ESL is in its infancy, only two booklets have been published by Tartu University ("Speaking Hands" and "The Dictionary of Christian Signs").

Funding

Social maintenance, pensions, and the cost of education up to high school level, at vocational schools and universities is covered by state and local communities. Estonian Sign Language interpretation costs are covered by local communities. Estonian Sign Language courses for parents of deaf children are financed by the Association of Parents of Hearing Impaired Children. ESL training courses for teachers of the deaf are financed by the local community. ESL training courses for interpreters are financed through pilot projects. ESL research work is financed by the state and/or by pilot projects.

4.3. Hungary[1]

Act No. XXVI of 1998 on the rights and equal opportunities of disabled people is a milestone in the history of Hungary. The Act states that disabled people have the right to barrier-free, perceivable/perceptible and safe environments in general.

The new Act No. CXXV of 2003 on equal treatment and promoting equal opportunities (hereinafter the "Act") increases the rights of people with disabilities. To a certain extent, its provisions have helped to harmonise and translate the 2000/78/EC Directive into the Hungarian legal system. The Act prescribes the right of equal treatment in the fields of employment, social security and health, housing, education, access to services and trade.

The government has issued its programme "New Dynamism for Hungary! The Programme of the Government of the Republic for a Free and Equitable Hungary 2004-2006". Within the chapter "Equitable Republic", the programme deals with the question of the situation of people with disabilities under the sub-title of the chance of an unimpaired life for people with special needs.

The government programme declares that equal opportunities are most important for people who can only live with help. For the government of the Republic, equal opportunities mean a more independent life.

Based on this programme, the minister responsible for equal opportunities stressed that one of the most important issues

---

1. In Hungary, the European Charter for Regional or Minority Languages (1992) entered into force on 1 March 1998.

in 2005 was to give priority to projects related to the implementation of sign language in Hungary.

The government also made efforts in the field of media to help eliminate the barriers of communication faced by sign language users. In this way, sign language interpreters have been, and are being, used in more newsreels, political programmes and several variety shows. Subtitling and sign language interpreters were both used recently in the regional TV newsreels. The minister responsible for equal opportunities has used a sign language interpreter during every official television appearance.

The Hungarian governmental administration views sign language as a means for the deaf to conduct interpersonal communication and respects the individual's right to the use of sign languages.

The Hungarian Government is committed to ensuring that a deaf person using sign language has the right to assistance from a sign language interpreter to access public information. Based on the Law on public education, children with special needs can use the sign language. The Decree of the Minister of Education No. 29 of 2002 also regulates special needs in higher education; on request a hearing impaired student should be provided with a sign language interpreter during oral examinations.

In the summer of 2002, the government took measures to set up a network of sign language interpreters. Since the beginning of 2003, six regional centres (Regional Sign Language Centres in Budapest, Debrecen, Györ, Eger, Pécs and Szekszárd) have provided deaf and hard-of-hearing people with relevant communicative assistance through the use of sign language interpreters.

The heads of the regional centres are qualified and proficient sign language interpreters. Their colleagues are employed on a full, part-time or free-lance basis. Dispatchers deal with the administration of needs of sign language users via post, telefax, e-mail as well as SMS. The service for the deaf and the hard-of-hearing is free of charge. Applications for sign language interpreters are prioritised by dispatchers based on the time received and the importance of needs. Over the past two years, demand for the service has been increasing and it is already beginning to reach its limit.

The regional services are committed to fulfilling the regulations of the Act No. XXVI of 1998 on the rights and equal opportunities of disabled people and its decrees in order to ensure services for all fields of public services. Based on a separate law, during administrative proceedings sign language users have the right to sign language interpreters who have been assigned as judicial experts.

Most demands of the service relate to training, education, health care and employment but there is also an increasing need for sign language interpretation during religious and leisure time activities, personal business, social problems as well as NGO activities.

So far the Ministry of Culture and National Heritage and the Hungarian Association of the Deaf and Hard of Hearing have co-operated in developing subtitling for hearing-impaired people. The Ministry provides financial means and the Association airs on average one evening programme (movie) a week with subtitling provided via teletext on the national channel (MTV1). The news broadcast at 19.30 on MTV 1 is subtitled via teletext and sign language interpreters translate regional newsreels at midday.

The plenary work of the Hungarian Parliament can be followed with a sign language interpreter on the other national channel (MTV 2).

The accreditation of sign language interpreters is finalised. The conditions of the training of sign language interpreters are based on the Decree of the Ministry of Education No. 28 of 2003, which lays down the requirements of qualification and examination including the preliminary stages. Several educational institutions have started their semesters of sign language interpretation. In the first half of 2005 the first sign language interpreters will graduate with an intermediate qualification of sign language. Within a period of two to three years, the increasing number of sign language interpreters will result in an improved level of professional expertise at regional centres.

In spring 2004, the Bureau of Sign Language Programme was set up as a professional background institution in order to ensure the success of the sign language project (development of the Hungarian Sign Language, the development of methodology of education as well as professional support for regional centres). The Bureau co-ordinates the programmes of sign language development in Hungary.

The National Council for Disability Affairs was set up by the Committee for Equal Opportunities in 2004. The President of this Council, a hard-of-hearing lawyer, worked with the committee on concepts of the regulation of the sign language in Hungary. The result of the work revealed that the modification of the Act No. XXVI of 1998 on the rights and equal opportunities of disabled people should be the best means (besides the possibilities of a separate sign language law or a communication law) to incorporate sign language into the Hungarian legal system. The committee also recommended the extension of its chapter on communication.

4.4. Iceland[1]

Media

Very little has changed regarding interpreted or text provision of news services: it is still rare to have such access, and even when provided, the quality tends to be low. Even where a news item is directly relevant to the deaf community (e.g. the discussion of cochlear implantation, the programme will generally remain un-subtitled. Where programmes are broadcast in the English language, Icelandic sub-titles are

---

1. Iceland signed the European Charter for Regional or Minority Languages (1992) on 7 May 1999.

provided. However, this is not the case for Icelandic programmes.

Education

In 1999, the Ministry of Education stated in the Icelandic basic curriculum that Icelandic Sign Language is the first language of deaf people, and Icelandic, the national language, is a second language for deaf Icelanders. As such, deaf Icelanders should learn Icelandic Sign Language as their first language and Icelandic as their second language. This basic curriculum does not apply to children under six years, so there is still work to do, as the critical period for language acquisition occurs prior to this age.

The basic curriculum also states that sign language has basic meaning for linguistic, cognitive and personality development for the deaf child. This obviously has serious implications for every deaf child's future.

Today, children aged 6-12 years can attend an "after-school service" with hearing students of the same age. This service is provided in conjunction with Hliðarskóli "twin-school for Vesturhilöarskóli", and is going well to date.

There have been some changes regarding provision at Kindergarten (pre-school) level since the Reykjavik Community took over. Today, the Kindergarten School for Deaf Children is at Sólborg. This school also caters for hearing children.

Interpretation

Problems still occur regarding the provision of Icelandic Sign Language interpreters: institutions are quick to argue that it is not their responsibility to cover interpreters' fees and that they do not have a budget to cover such costs. The IDO are currently campaigning for interpretation for elderly deaf people when they participate in social activities at a day centre for elderly people in Geröuberg.

Icelandic Sign Language interpreter training

The summers of 1997 and 1998 saw two groups of students graduate from the University of Iceland. This training was supported by the Communication Centre for the Deaf and Hard of Hearing and the Ministry of Education.

4.5. Latvia[1]

Sign language has no officially recognised status, is neither used as the first language in education of deaf people, nor recognised as the main means of communication between deaf persons and others. There are government measures to encourage media to make their services accessible to persons with disabilities but no government measures to encourage other forms of public information to make their services accessible to persons with disabilities. The following service is provided to facilitate information and communication between persons with disabilities and others: sign language interpretation is available only for major events.[2]

4.6. Lithuania[3]

The Parliament of the Republic of Lithuania passed the Law of Social Integration of the Disabled in 1991 following the Constitution of the Republic of Lithuania, seeking to implement the rights of disabled people consolidated in international acts and acknowledging that the integration of disabled people into society and public life is one of the indicators of civilisation. It is stated in the law that sign language is a native language of the deaf.

---

1. Latvia has not signed the European Charter for Regional or Minority Languages (1992).
2. Contribution of the Latvian Association of the Deaf in the report "Government Implementation of the Standard Rules as seen by Member Organizations of the World Federation of the Deaf – WFD", Dimitris Michailakis 1997.
3. Lithuania has not signed the European Charter for Regional or Minority Languages (1992).

Following the Law of the Social Integration of the Disabled and implementing the Activity Programme of the Government of the Republic of Lithuania during 1997-2000, the Ministry of Social Security and Labour jointly with the Ministry of Education and Science and the Lithuanian Union of the Deaf have elaborated the National Programme of Using Sign Language. The Ministry of Social Security and Labour is obliged to co-ordinate and administrate the implementation of the programme. The objective of the programme is to establish an effective sign language corresponding to the conditions of the Republic of Lithuania and international standards, adjusted to all living occasions. Through implementing the programme it is planned to secure the services of sign language interpretation; to research the demand for using the services of sign language interpretation in state, public and communal institutions; to stimulate, support and allow research on Lithuanian Sign Language, to nourish it, to create and keep the traditions and the culture of the deaf. The programme was implemented for six years: from 1998 to 2003.

It is expected that the implementation of the programme will lead to changes in educating deaf children, youth and adults with the help of the Lithuanian Sign Language in special education institutions. More talented students will have the possibilities not only of attending general or special education institutions, but also of striving for a higher education. Persons with impaired hearing not having intellectual disabilities will have the same possibilities as the hearing. The possibilities of getting different information through television, conferences, seminars, cultural and sport events will help the deaf to become informed citizens. This will be of great social and moral use.

The implementation of the programme is financed from the state budget, assigning the finances to the Lithuanian Council for the Affairs of the Disabled under the Government of the Republic of Lithuania for the implementation of the Programme of Medical, Social and Vocational Rehabilitation.

The National Programme of Using Sign Language is implemented by the Lithuanian Union of the Deaf jointly with the

Ministry of Education and Science. One basic means of the implementation of the programme is to establish the centres of sign language interpreters in the counties. The funds for the establishment of these centres are projected in the National Programme of Medical, Social and Vocational Rehabilitation. The funds for the maintenance of the centres are to be planned by county administrations in their budgets. The aim of the centres is to design the most favourable conditions for society and deaf persons to communicate by sign language and for deaf persons to receive education and information through sign language. The goals of the centres are to provide services of sign language interpretation, to research the demand of using the sign language interpretation service in autonomous, state, public and communal institutions, to care about training and upgrading qualification of sign language interpreters.

When implementing the programme, an important task is to secure the provision of a sign language interpretation service. Therefore, considerable attention is paid to the sign language interpreters' training programme and the training itself. The interpreters training programme has been started and a group formed to study sign language, the aim being to reach the standard of qualified interpreters in sign language.

Sign language courses are also being organised for pedagogues of schools of the deaf and hard-of-hearing. With their help the implementation of the bilingual education method is stimulated in the institutions of the deaf; new signs such as religious, political, etc. are consolidated. Methodical support to educational institutions is provided.

The project "Security of Native Language for Deaf Children", which won the support in the European Community Access Phare Programme, is being implemented. Implementing the project, a more positive image of the deaf has been formed in society with the help of the media.

Educational aids are adjusted to the deaf. Considerable attention is paid to research related to sign language. Subject dictionaries of the sign language such as "The Signs of

97

Religion", "The Signs of Geography" have been prepared and edited. Also five volumes of the Dictionary of the Sign Language have been edited. A videotape of the dictionary of the sign language has been created. This is a visual educational aid to teach people with hearing impairment the sign language. Seeking to standardise the signs used in educational programmes videotape "The Primer of the Sign Language" for deaf children has been created. Deaf children and pedagogues in all education institutions of the deaf will use the same signs; this will facilitate teaching the sign language. Deaf students studying in different universities, colleges or art schools of the country are supported. It is sought to design as favourable conditions as possible for the deaf to reach a higher or special education.

4.7. Poland[1]

Sign language is recognised as the official language for deaf people, used as the first language in the education of deaf people and recognised as the main means of communication between deaf persons and others. There are government measures to encourage media and other forms of public information to make their services accessible to persons with disabilities. The following service is provided in order to facilitate information and communication between persons with disabilities and other persons: sign language interpretation being available only for major events.[2]

The Polish governmental administration treats sign languages as means for the deaf to engage in interpersonal communication. It respects the individual right to use sign languages and promotes Polish Sign Language. Polish is the only official language recognised in the Polish Constitution of April 1997 (Article 27). But the provision that "Polish shall be

---

1. Poland signed the European Charter for Regional or Minority Languages (1992) on 12 May 2003.
2. Country report on Rule 5 "Accessibility" of the UN Standard Rules on the Equalization of Opportunities for Persons with Disabilities, submitted in August 2001.

the official language in the Republic of Poland" "shall not infringe upon national minority rights resulting from ratified international agreements".

The Polish Constitution, although it does not contain any special provision recognising sign language, states that "public authorities shall provide, in accordance with the statute, aid to disabled persons to ensure their subsistence, adaptation to work and social communication" (Article 69). In the resolution passed on 1 August 1997 the Polish Seym (the lower chamber of the Polish Parliament) recognised that persons with disabilities have the right, inter alia, to life in an environment free from functional barriers, including, for example, the possibility of interpersonal communication.

Regulations of the Act of 27 August 1997 on Vocational and Social Rehabilitation and Employment of Disabled Persons enable practical implementation of this right providing that resources of the State Fund for Rehabilitation of Disabled Persons (PFRON) may be allocated to co-financing of removing barriers, for example, in communication. Thanks to the regulations of this Act it is possible to work out various target programmes enabling deaf persons for example to take advantage of electronic equipment for wireless communication in the education process or of sign language interpreters' services. One of the target programmes, which has been implemented for a few years, provides necessary aid for people with impaired hearing who study at a university or want to study and have to pass the entrance exams.

The other target programme enables financing of the training costs of sign language interpreters and for employees of various institutions who have to use sign language in their work, as well as for adult disabled persons who suffer from a dysfunction of the organs of hearing and speech.

In case payment is required it is also possible for a deaf person to get financial support from the PFRON resources for the service of a sign language interpreter.

Deaf children have the right to education in sign language and to use this language in school. But teaching of sign language is not obligatory and each school may choose the methods of communication with deaf children. So deaf children have been taught in the following methods: oral, oral with the use of phono-gestures, oral and sign, sign or total communication. The total communication, which uses all the methods mentioned before, has become very popular in Poland recently as it gives a child with a hearing impairment better opportunities for integration into society.

The teachers of deaf children have the right to make use of sign language during the teaching process. To help them to aquire the skills, the Ministry of National Education has financed or co-financed their training and study materials for many years. Over 400 teachers from special schools have taken courses in Polish Sign Language run by the Polish Association of the Deaf.

The Ministry of National Education fosters and promotes broadening and disseminating the knowledge about communication of the deaf, by organising or co-financing conferences in this field. This ministry has also issued various study and didactic materials for the learning and teaching of Polish Sign Language.

Regulations of the Minister of National Education in the field of the educational system cover provisions concerning the adjustment of school and examination requirements to the needs and abilities of children and youth with hearing impairments, including the use of sign language.

The Polish legislation provides that a deaf person has the right to assistance of a sign language interpreter during judicial proceedings. It is for the court or other competent bodies running the criminal or civil proceedings to call a sign language interpreter, if they need to examine a deaf or deaf-mute person and it is not sufficient to communicate with him or her in writing.

Considering the fact that the assistance of a sign language interpreter may be essential in many situations of life of a deaf person who uses sign language and has difficulties in communicating in another way, the Polish public authorities appreciate the importance of sign language interpreters and of the Polish Association of the Deaf, which has run the training courses for sign language interpreters, preparing study materials and dictionaries based on unified signs of Polish Sign Language and participating in their publication. Since 1967 this association has trained about 2,800 people and to date 835 people have been registered by the association as sign language interpreters, but they do not have certificates of their professional skills.

It is worth mentioning that also some universities enable non-deaf students to attend courses in Polish Sign Language, for example the University of Warsaw as from the academic year 1998-99.

At the end of 1998, sign language interpreter was recognised as a profession in Poland and included in the occupational classification. It constitutes the basis for the establishment and enforcement of the schema for professional education of sign language interpreters within the general system of education of various professions. The Polish Association of the Deaf plans to create a new educational centre for the training of sign language interpreters, which will issue the appropriate certificates enabling to practice this profession.

The Polish Association of the Deaf, commenting on the matter of the status of sign language, maintains that the population of the deaf in Poland should be considered as a minority language and Polish Sign Language needs legal reinforcement.

The Polish governmental administration responsible for the social policy concerning persons with disabilities is rather in favour of the opinion that there is an essential difference between the role of sign languages and the historical regional or minority languages. The latter contribute to the maintenance of territorial integrity and national sovereignty, the diversity of tradition, cultural wealth and heritage of the par-

101

ticular groups of national minorities, while sign languages should be helpful in communication, education, development and full integration of the deaf into the society in which they live with the same tradition and culture, but should not separate them from their national society. Sign languages should be seen as a tool for people with disabilities. The use of sign languages should be promoted through appropriate measures.

4.8. Romania[1]

Sign language is recognised as the main means of communication between deaf persons and others. There are government measures encouraging media and other forms of public information to make their services accessible. Sign language interpretation is available for any purpose in order to facilitate information and communication between persons with disabilities and other persons.[2]

---

1. Romania signed the European Charter for Regional or Minority Languages (1992) on 17 July 1995.
2. Government Action on Disability Policy, A global Survey, Dimitris Michailakis, 1997.

CHAPTER 5 – POSITION OF
THE EUROPEAN UNION OF THE DEAF (EUD)

The European Union of the Deaf (EUD)[1], a European non-profit making NGO whose membership comprises national associations of deaf people in each of the EU member states, is in favour of an additional protocol on sign languages to the European Charter for Regional or Minority Languages.

On 17-18 February 2001, the European Union of the Deaf (EUD) organised a Seminar on Sign Languages in Lund, Sweden. Delegates from all European Union member states were present, along with representatives from outside the European Union - Estonia, Iceland, Norway and Russia. At that seminar, each national association's official delegate provided an overview of the status of sign languages in their country. These reports followed up on the research carried out during the EUD Sign Languages Project 1997.

In March 2001, the EUD published its paper "Update on the status of sign languages in the European Union". According to the EUD, in many countries the official sign language(s) is/are recognised to some extent, but sign languages are rarely officially recognised as such in national constitutions or in legislation as the preferred language of the deaf community living in the country.

According to the EUD, the following countries within the Council of Europe have a constitutional reference to their sign languages.

– Czech Republic (1988) – Czech Sign Language

---

1. Established in 1985, EUD is the only organisation representing the interests of deaf people in the European Union, in consultation and co-operation with its member National Deaf Associations.

- Finland (1995) – sign language users
- Greece (2000) – Greek Sign Language
- Portugal (1997) – Portuguese Sign Language
- Slovak Republic (1995) – deaf sign language users

Despite those claims by NGOs and certain MEPs, Finland and Portugal seem to be the only two European countries that have constitutional references to sign languages. However, Greece, the Czech Republic and the Slovak Republic do recognise sign language in legislation (but so do other European countries).

According to the EUD, the following countries within the Council of Europe have passed laws that refer to sign languages/sign language users in a direct or indirect way: Denmark, France, Italy, Ireland, Lithuania, Norway, Switzerland, Sweden, Ukraine, United Kingdom.

In all European countries deaf associations and their members and allies have continued to campaign vigorously for the recognition of sign languages as fully-fledged languages, on equal footing with the spoken languages of their country/region. The campaign for increased recognition of sign languages has been backed up by research demonstrating that sign languages are languages in their own right, with independent lexicons and grammar systems.

According to the EUD, small but profound changes are also taking place in deaf education: more and more deaf children are being taught bilingually, even though in many countries this still remains experimental and is the exception rather than the rule. Only in Scandinavian countries are deaf children entitled to receive a bilingual education, while in other countries, it is up to the child's parents to decide. Nevertheless, the oral method of education is slowly but surely losing ground to the bilingual approach. More demands are being placed on teachers of the deaf – including those who have been working with deaf children for years – to acquire their national sign language in order to be able to communicate effectively with their pupils. In some countries it is a prerequisite for teachers who want to work with deaf children to know sign language, before they can start teaching deaf children.

Another trend that is seen in the country reports is that more and more hearing people are interested in learning a sign language. Sometimes the demand is so great that there is not an adequate supply of appropriate courses on offer. The consequence is that in many cases the quality of sign language courses cannot be guaranteed or controlled, as often, unqualified sign language instructors are used to teach sign language courses.

The EUD considers that the lack of adequate training and resources for sign language instructors pose problems in many countries, especially if they are deaf, since deaf people have generally had less educational opportunities than their non-deaf counterparts. There is also a wide diversity in the standards and level of sign language instruction/training. But in many countries serious efforts are being undertaken to streamline courses and standards, and to improve co-operation and co-ordination among the different "actors" in this field. Furthermore, in some countries universities or institutes of higher education have begun to offer courses for those who want to learn sign language as a foreign language and/or those who want to become a qualified sign language interpreter. Thus standards are being raised and sign language training for would-be sign language interpreters are no longer confined to evening classes.

At its 24th session, The Hague, 26-29 June 2001, the Council of Europe's Committee on the Rehabilitation and Integration of People with disabilities (CD-P-RR) initiated the process of reviewing the EUD country reports on the status of sign languages by asking delegations to check and amend the information provided in that document, or provide such information, if necessary. The results of that review are set out in chapters 3 and 4 of this report.

CHAPTER 6 – CONCLUSIONS: THE RECOGNITION OF SIGN LANGUAGES IN CONSTITUTIONS AND LEGISLATION

6.1. Constitutional recognition of sign language

Despite other claims by NGOs and certain MEPs, Finland and Portugal seem to be the only two European countries that have constitutional references to sign languages.[1]

There are about 8,000 deaf people in Finland, 5,000 of which use sign language as their first language. It is estimated that the number of sign language users in Finland amounts to about 15,000. The corner stone of the Finnish Sign Language status was laid in 1995, when the section regarding language rights of the renewed provisions of the fundamental law of the Finnish constitution provided legal protection for sign language users. Recognising the status of the sign language in the constitution was a big step towards achieving linguistic equality, and it had a significance of principle for the sign language using community. People using sign language were conceived now for the first time as a linguistic and cultural group. An international comparison shows that Finland was one of the first countries in the world where the national sign language was recognised on a constitutional level.

The modified constitution obliges public authorities to take active measures in order to ensure that sign language users have the opportunity to use their own language and to develop their own culture. The obligation of making sure means first and foremost enacting laws, and some steps forward have already been taken in that respect after 1995. In

---

1. Note that some countries have no written constitution, so constitutional recognition of their sign language(s) is not possible (e.g. the United Kingdom).

these new legal provisions, an analogy has usually been drawn between the sign language and the two minority languages spoken in Finland: the Sami and the Romany languages.

Section 17 Right to one's language and culture of the Constitution of Finland says "The national languages of Finland are Finnish and Swedish. The right of everyone to use his or her own language, either Finnish or Swedish, before courts of law and other authorities, and to receive official documents in that language, shall be guaranteed by an Act. The public authorities shall provide for the cultural and societal needs of the Finnish-speaking and Swedish-speaking populations of the country on an equal basis. The Sami, as an indigenous people, as well as the Roma and other groups, have the right to maintain and develop their own language and culture. Provisions on the right of the Sami to use the Sami language before the authorities are laid down by an Act. The rights of persons using sign language and of persons in need of interpretation or translation aid owing to disability shall be guaranteed by an Act."

Article 74 Education of the Constitution of Portugal (as amended in 1997) says in paragraph 2 g) "In the implementation of its policy for education, it is the duty of the state to promote and support access by citizens with disabilities to education andsupport special education where necessary." Paragraph 2. h) says "In the implementation of its policy for education, it is the duty of the state to protect and develop Portuguese Sign Language, as a cultural expression and instrument of access to education and equality of opportunity."

6.2. Recognition of sign language (users) in legislation

The following table shows a list of European countries which have passed laws that refer to sign languages and/or sign language users in a direct or indirect way (reference to 'barrier-free' communication is an example of an indirect way of recognising sign language).

108

Summary of recent developments with regard to the recognition of sign language in legislation:

As from 3 July 2003 Belgian-French Sign Language has been recognised as the language of the deaf by the Health Minister of the French community in **Belgium**. This recognition implies that Belgian-French Sign Language can be used to train deaf teachers and interpreters and to use Belgian-French Sign Language in mainstream education next to French. In addition, Belgian-French Sign Language is referred to in certain legal texts – such as the Decree on Basic Education. On 21 October 2003, the Decree of the Recognition of Sign Language was voted at unanimity by the Parliament of the French-speaking Community of Belgium. It is a great political victory of the deaf society because all political parties (majority and opposition) promised their commitment to the issue and to work together for the recognition of a minority language. Sign Language will therefore become the fourth national language, along with French, Flemish-Dutch and German.

In the **Czech Republic,** the equality of sign language with other languages is proclaimed by Law no. 155 of 11 June 1998 (Sign Language Act). The law provides that sign language shall be the means of communication for the deaf in the Czech Republic. It further provides that the deaf are entitled to the use of sign language, to be educated by means of sign language, and to be taught it. The law also stipulates that in visits to medical practitioners, dealings with the administration and judicial procedure, deaf people are entitled to the provision of an interpreter without payment. Deaf students engaged in tertiary studies are also entitled to a non-paying interpretation service.

In **Denmark,** Danish Sign Language has been recognised as a language by the government and the public authorities since 1991. It is considered as the primary language of deaf children. Sign language is recommended as the primary language for instruction and communication in the education of deaf children.

Country	Legislation referring to sign language (users)
Belgium	Decree on the right to sign language interpretation 1995,[1] Decree on Basic Education 1998,[2] Decree of the Recognition of Sign Language 20032
Czech Republic	Sign Language Act of 11 June 1998 (Law no. 155), Czech Television Act, Act on Radio and Television Broadcasting
Denmark	Education Act 1991
Finland	Law on Administrative Procedure (598/1982), Criminal Investigations Act (1987), Services and Assistance for the Disabled Act (380/1987), Support and Assistance for the Disabled Decree (759/1987), Acts on the position and rights of patients and clients in the social and health sector (1992 and 2000), Law on the Research Institute for the Languages of Finland (591/1996), Decree on the Research Institute for the Languages of Finland (758/1996), Law on Basic Education (628/1998), Law on Upper Secondary School (629/1998), Law on Vocational Education (630/1998), Act on Broadcasting Yleisradio Oy (746/1998), Law on the Position and Rights of the Social Welfare Client (812/2000), Nationality Act (2003), Language Act (2003), Administrative procedure Act (2003), Administrative Judicial procedure Act (2003)
France	Law on Equal Rights and Opportunities, Participation and Citizenship of People with Disabilities of 1 March 2004
Germany	Code of Social Law No IX 2001, Act on Equal Opportunities for Disabled Persons 2002
Hungary	Act I of 1996 on radio and television, Act XXVI of 1998 on rights and equal opportunities of disabled people, Act CXXV of 2003 on equal treatment and promoting equal opportunity, Decree no. 28/2003 on equal opportunities, non-discrimination and universal access for persons with disabilities

1. French-speaking Region of Brussels-Capital.
2. The Walloon Region of Belgium.

110

Country	Legislation referring to sign language (users)
Ireland	Education Act 1998
Italy	Law No. 104/1992, Law No. 17/1999
Lithuania	Law of Social Integration of the disabled 1991, 1995 Act concerning the proclamation of 1996 as the year of the disabled
Norway	Primary Education Act 1997, Education Act 1998 as amended in 1999
Poland	Act of 27 August 1997 on Vocational and Social Rehabilitation and Employment of Disabled Persons
Portugal	Act No. 31-A/98 as amended by Act No. 8/2002, Law 38 1999
Slovak Republic	Act 149/1995 on Sign Language for the Deaf
Slovenia	Use of Slovenian Sign Language Act 2002
Spain	Royal Decree 20/60/1995, Royal Decree 696/1995, Act no. 51/2003 on equal opportunities, non-discrimination and universal access for persons with disabilities
Sweden	Comprehensive Schools Act SFS 1997:599, Education Act 1998;1100, amendment November 1999, Health and Medical Service Act 1982 as amended
Switzerland	Federal Law of 19 June 1959 on invalidity insurance as amended, Federal Law of 13 December 2002
United Kingdom	Police and Criminal Evidence Act (1984), Justice of the Peace Act (1979), NHS and Community Care Act (1990), Broadcasting Act (1996), Disability Discrimination Act (1995), Representation of the People Act (2000), Draft Disability Discrimination Bill (3 December 2003)

In **Germany,** with the Act on Equal Opportunities for Disabled Persons, which entered into force on 1 May 2002, the ban on discrimination contained in the Basic Law over and above social law is implemented across the whole public law area in Germany. Following the Act on Combating Unemployment among People with Severe Disabilities and Book IX of the Social Code on Integration and Rehabilitation of People with Disabilities, it represents the third significant act in the field of disability policy adopted in the years 2000-2002. The Act serves to ensure the equal rights of disabled persons in all fields of life and to put them into practice in everyday life. It is a matter of eliminating the obstacles standing in the way of equal opportunities.

The core of the Act on Equal Opportunities for Disabled Persons is the creation of comprehensively understood barrier-free environments. Barrier-free environments are conditional on comprehensive access and unrestricted use of all designed environments. The goal of general barrier-free environments includes the development of barrier-free communication such as using sign language interpreters or barrier-free electronic media. In addition three ordinances entered into force in July 2002 which obliged federal authorities to ensure barrier-free environments in the broadest sense of the word. Hearing- or speech-impaired persons have the right when defending their own rights in administrative procedures with all Federal authorities to communicate in German Sign Language with signs supporting spoken language or via other suitable communication aids. The authorities have to meet the cost.

The Parliament of the **Republic of Lithuania** passed the Law on Social Integration of the Disabled in 1991. In this law it is stated that sign language is a native language of the deaf. The 1995 Act concerning the proclamation of 1996 as the Year of the Disabled led to the official recognition of sign language as the official language of deaf people.

In the **Netherlands,** although the constitution does not regulate the national language(s), various laws contain stipulations concerning the use of the Dutch language and the Friesian language. Since 1995 the General Administrative Law Act has regulated that administrative bodies must use the Dutch language and more recently legislation on education has defined the language in which education is to be provided.

In **Poland,** although the constitution does not contain any special provision recognising sign language, it states however that "public authorities shall provide, in accordance with the statute, aid to disabled persons to ensure their subsistence, adaptation to work and social communication" (Article 69). In the resolution passed on 1 August 1997, the Polish Seym (the lower chamber of the Polish Parliament) recognised that persons with disabilities have the right, inter alia, to life in an environment free from functional barriers, including e.g. the possibility of interpersonal communication.

In the **Slovak Republic,** Slovak Sign Language, though protected by Law No. 149 of 26 June 1995, which secures the right to use, receive instruction and be informed in it, is not recognised as a minority language.

The constitution of the **Republic of Slovenia** regulates human rights and fundamental liberties and ensures equality before the law, which represents, together with the Declaration of the rights of disabled people, the fundamental legal basis for the preparation of the statute on sign language. In 2002, Slovenia adopted the Use of Slovenian Sign Language Act, which recognises the right of deaf people to use Slovenian Sign Language and the right to a sign language interpreter. This removes the basic communication barrier between hearing people and hearing-impaired people and will improve the prospects for deaf people to acquire appropriate education and appropriate social and political involvement in society.

In **Spain,** the Ministry of Labour and Social Affairs prepared a comprehensive report on the repercussions that the progressive recognition of sign languages could have in its area, undertaking its study in the fields of non-regular training, employment and social services. The document establishes that the main fields of action for the government to progressively implement the recognition of sign languages would be the following:

- Implantation of sign languages in the public administration by means of interpretation services offered progressively for deaf users who demand this form of communication, and by fostering widespread sign language training for the general information service staff.
- Gradual implantation of a policy encouraging bilingualism among the deaf.

As priority steps, the government undertakes to carry out:
- An analysis of the social and labour situation of the deaf in Spain;
- Measures leading to the training of sign language interpreters;
- Training action for sign language interpretation aimed at civil servants of the government's general administration.

The National Action Plan for Social Inclusion (2001-2003) included measures to support the use of sign languages as a communication tool for the deaf, fundamentally in their dealings with public administrations.

Sweden has officially recognised sign language since 1981: "The Government Commission on Integration points out that the profoundly deaf have to be bilingual to function among themselves and in society. Bilingualism on their part, according to the commission, means that they have to be fluent in their visual/gestural sign language, and in the language that society surrounds them with, Swedish." (Government Bill 1980/1981:100).

In **Switzerland,** the status of sign languages was raised in the Swiss Parliament in 1994, when the Committee on Education, Science and Culture issued a formal proposal on sign language inviting the Federal Council (government) to recognise it for the purpose of integrating the deaf and hard of hearing and encourage it alongside the spoken language in education, training, research and communication. The Federal Council accepted the proposal. It is not intended to give sign languages official language status in Switzerland but to grant them a greater role in integration policies and above all to establish legal provisions to encourage their use. Following acceptance of the proposal, sign languages are taken into consideration when new laws are drafted or existing ones revised.

The **United Kingdom** has no written constitution. The United Kingdom regulated the use of sign language in several legislative acts (the Police and Criminal Evidence Act (1984), the Justice of the Peace Act (1979), the NHS and Community Care Act (1990), the Broadcasting Act (1996), the Disability Discrimination Act (1995) and the Representation of the People Act (2000)). For an estimated 70,000 deaf people sign language is their preferred language for participation in everyday life. British Sign Language is a visual-gestural language with its own vocabulary, grammar and syntax. On 18 March 2003, the British Government recognised British Sign Language as a language in its own right. Deaf people recently won formal government recognition of British Sign Language requiring education authorities to provide better opportunities for deaf children to learn communication skills.

APPENDIX I

Recommendation 1492 (2001)[1]
of the Parliamentary Assembly of the
Council of Europe "Rights of national minorities"

1.   The Assembly again stresses the importance of effectively protecting the rights of minorities in Europe. It considers that adequate protection for persons belonging to national minorities and their communities is an integral part of the protection of human rights and is the only way in which states can reduce ethnic tensions that might give rise to more widespread conflicts.

2.   The Assembly condemns the denial of the existence of minorities and of minority rights in several Council of Europe member states and the fact that many minorities in Europe are not afforded adequate protection.

3.   The Assembly recognises that the majority has obligations towards the minority and, on the other hand, the minority has the responsibility to participate in political and public life of the country in which it lives and to contribute, along with the majority, to the democratic cohesion and pluralism of the states to which it has offered its allegiance.

4.   The Assembly notes that it is essential that the majority becomes more familiar with the languages and cultures of

1. *Assembly debate* on 23 January 2001 (3rd Sitting) (see Doc. 8920, report of the Committee on Legal Affairs and Human Rights, rapporteur: Mr Bindig, Doc. 8939; the opinion of the Political Affairs Committee, rapporteur: Mr Gjellerod, Doc. 8943; the opinion of the Committee on Migration, Refugees and Demography, rapporteur: Mr Tabajdi; and Doc. 8941, the opinion of the Committee on Culture and Education, rapporteur: Mr de Puig). *Text adopted by the Assembly* on 23 January 2001 (3rd Sitting).

national minorities and that the authorities, with the help of non-governmental organisations, endeavour to make minority cultures known.

5. The Assembly once more calls on all its member states to safeguard what could be considered to be the minimum rights of national minorities, as set out in the Framework Convention for the Protection of National Minorities (ETS No. 157). It believes that the protection of minorities is essential to the implementation of fundamental human rights, stability, democratic security and peace on the European continent. It also points out that the price to be paid for failing to respond positively to the needs of national minorities may be an escalation in social tension, an increase in the number of asylum seekers, reluctance to reinforce unity between the member states of the Council of Europe and a climate of insecurity which would be detrimental to trade and investment.

6. Andorra, Belgium, France and Turkey have to date neither signed nor ratified the Framework Convention for the Protection of National Minorities and this means that it cannot take full effect across the continent. These countries have significant minorities, which ought to be protected, and whose rights are not officially recognised. Other countries – Georgia, Greece, Iceland, Latvia, Luxembourg, the Netherlands and Portugal – have signed but not yet ratified the framework convention.

7. The Assembly recalls its Recommendation 1201 (1993), in which it asked the Committee of Ministers to draw up an additional protocol to the European Convention on Human Rights on the rights of minorities, and expressed a wish for Council of Europe member states to base their legislation and policies concerning minorities on the draft protocol set out in the appendix to that recommendation, which contained the most acceptable definition at European level of a "national minority".

8. The Assembly also points out that the political undertakings and standards set out in the draft additional protocol appended to the above recommendation have been raised to

the status of legal obligations in friendship treaties drawn up between various member states of the Council of Europe. These treaty obligations might eventually acquire customary status at regional level.

9. To date, Albania, Andorra, Belgium, Bulgaria, Estonia, Georgia, Greece, Ireland, Latvia, Lithuania, Moldova, Poland, Portugal, the Russian Federation, San Marino, Slovakia and Turkey have neither signed nor ratified the European Charter for Regional or Minority Languages (ETS No. 148).

10. The Assembly notes that the Charter of Fundamental Rights of the European Union, as accepted at the Summit meeting in Nice in December 2000, does not tackle the question of minority rights and limits itself to declaring in its Article 22 that "the Union shall respect cultural, religious and linguistic diversity".

11. The Assembly recognises that immigrant populations whose members are citizens of the state in which they reside constitute special categories of minorities, and recommends that a specific Council of Europe instrument should be applied to them.

12. The Assembly therefore recommends that the Committee of Ministers:

i.   call upon member states to show a more generous attitude in applying their specific minority policies and in the implementation of Council of Europe instruments in the field of minorities;

ii.   call upon member states to improve and, where needed, further develop international co-operation in minority rights protection, both in their bilateral relations and at the level of European international organisations;

iii.   ask the four states which have not signed the Framework Convention for the Protection of National Minorities to bring their constitution and their legislation into harmony with the European standards in force in order to remove any obstacle to the signature and ratification of the convention;

iv. ask the states mentioned in paragraph 6 of this convention to sign and/or ratify as soon as possible and without reservations and declarations the Framework Convention for the Protection of National Minorities, and ask those which have already ratified it to implement it and to revoke their reservations and declarations;

v. encourage those states which have not yet done so to ratify the European Charter for Regional or Minority Languages, and encourage states parties and future states parties to apply it properly;

vi. increase the human and financial resources of the general directorates of the Council of Europe concerned by the application of the two aforementioned instruments;

vii. ask member states to sign and to ratify as soon as possible Protocol No. 12 to the European Convention on Human Rights, in the hope that persons belonging to national minorities will be able to have their specific rights confirmed by the European Court of Human Rights;

viii. call upon the Committee of Ministers to give a high priority to the discussion and adoption of the opinions and reports issued by the Consultative Committee of the Framework Convention for the Protection of National Minorities and the Committee of Experts of the European Charter for Regional or Minority Languages, and create a suitable procedure for their speedy publication and general dissemination;

ix. strengthen the monitoring mechanisms within the Council of Europe and apply the same principles and standards to all member states;

x. begin drafting an additional protocol to the Framework Convention for the Protection of National Minorities giving the European Court of Human Rights or a general judicial authority of the Council of Europe the power to give advisory opinions concerning the interpretation of the framework convention;

xi. begin drafting a protocol to the European Convention on Human Rights on the rights of national minorities, drawing on the principles contained in Recommendation 1201 (1993), and endeavouring to include therein the definition of national minority adopted in the same recommendation;

xii. attach to the Council of Europe Commissioner for Human Rights a person with special responsibility for issues concerning the protection of minorities' rights, making suitable financial provision for this purpose;

xiii. give the various sign languages utilised in Europe a protection similar to that afforded by the European Charter for Regional or Minority Languages, possibly by means of the adoption of a recommendation to member states;

xiv. publish the reports submitted by the Committee of Experts of the European Charter for Regional or Minority Languages.

APPENDIX II

Reply of the Committee of Ministers of the Council of Europe to Parliamentary Assembly Recommendation 1492 (2001)

(Decision adopted by the Deputies on 13 June 2002 at their 799th meeting)

The Deputies adopted the following reply to Parliamentary Assembly Recommendation 1492 (2001) on the rights of national minorities:

"The Committee of Ministers carefully examined Parliamentary Assembly Recommendation 1492 on the rights of national minorities. Before drafting a reply, it saw fit to request the opinions of the Advisory Committee on the Framework Convention for the Protection of National Minorities, the Steering Committee for Human Rights (CDDH), the Committee of Experts of the European Charter for Regional or Minority Languages, the Committee on the Rehabilitation and Integration of People with disabilities (Partial Agreement CD-P-RR) and the Commissioner for Human Rights. The various opinions in question are appended. Reference is made to these opinions for more detailed explanations of the stands taken in this reply.

The Committee of Ministers shares the Assembly's view that effective protection for the rights of persons belonging to national minorities in Europe is of great importance to the implementation of human rights and fundamental freedoms and to stability, democratic security and peace in Europe. Like the Assembly, it stresses that such protection is an integral part of the protection of human rights. The Committee of Ministers would point out that, to date, the Framework Convention is the only legally binding multilateral instrument in Europe for the protection of national minorities in general and is therefore a key tool for action in this field.

Bearing in mind Articles 2 and 18 of the Framework Convention, which refer to international co-operation in this field, the Committee of Ministers shares the Assembly's concern that international, multilateral and bilateral co-operation should be stepped up in the area of protection of national minorities. With regard to co-operation among member states at the level of the Council of Europe, the Committee of Ministers draws attention to activities such as the regular meetings (since 1994) of the Governmental Offices for national minorities, the programme of Confidence Building measures, the more recent projects under the Stability Pact for South - Eastern Europe or the Venice Commission's legal work in this field. It likewise agrees with the Assembly that more determined action on the part of member states at national level is needed to implement the Council of Europe instruments in the field of protection of national minorities.[1]

Like the Assembly, the Committee of Ministers considers that states should be encouraged to remove the obstacles that exist at national level in order to sign and/or ratify as soon as possible the Framework Convention. For the reasons stated in their respective opinions by the CDDH and the Advisory Committee on the Framework Convention, the Committee of Ministers considers that States Parties to the Framework Convention should be judicious in their use of reservations or declarations. The Committee of Ministers agrees that states should be encouraged to ratify and implement the European Charter for Regional or Minority Languages and sign and ratify Protocol No.12 (general prohibition of discrimination) to the European Convention on Human Rights.[2]

---

1. See notes on page 157 (3rd Sitting).

The Committee of Ministers recognises the need to speed up, at all levels, the monitoring procedures relating to the Framework Convention for the Protection of National Minorities and the European Charter for Regional or Minority Languages. The Committee of Ministers also notes the importance of making public the results of monitoring exercises quickly and disseminating them widely and recalls that the bodies entrusted with the monitoring of these treaties can highlight examples of best practices where appropriate.[3]

The Committee of Ministers likewise welcomes the fact that there has been a steady increase in the volume of work relating to this supervision and acknowledges that it is important that sufficient resources should be made available to ensure that these convention-related responsibilities can be shouldered. The Committee of Ministers would point out that the increase in resources and the strengthening of monitoring systems, including with respect to the activities of the Commissioner for Human Rights related to the protection of national minorities, must be considered in the context of the Organisation's overall needs, in the light of the priority afforded to the protection of national minorities. In this context possible re-activation of the intergovernmental work carried out by the Committee of experts on issues relating to the protection of national minorities (DH-MIN) could be considered further.[4]

With regard to the proposal for an additional protocol to the European Convention on Human Rights concerning the rights of national minorities, which would include the definition of national minority contained in Assembly Recommendation 1201 (1993), the Committee of Ministers considers that it is somewhat premature to reopen the debate on this project. The Committee of Ministers would stress in this connection that, when Protocol No. 12 to the European Convention on Human Rights comes into force, any discrimination against a member of a national minority, including discrimination based on association with such a minority, will be covered by the general prohibition on discrimination.[5]

125

With regard to the Assembly's recommendation that an additional protocol be prepared to the Framework Convention for the Protection of National Minorities, giving the European Court of Human Rights or a general judicial authority of the Council of Europe the power to submit advisory opinions on the interpretation of the Framework Convention, the Committee of Ministers refers, on the substance of the issue, to the negative view of the CDDH, to the opinion of the Advisory Committee on the Framework Convention, stating that such an additional protocol would be premature, and to the conclusion of the European Court (Appendix 6 of the current reply) according to which it "is in principle willing to assume an interpretative role in the field of minority protection", if such a protocol were to be established. For the reasons stated in these opinions, the Committee of Ministers does not consider it appropriate to give the Court new powers by means of an additional protocol to the Framework Convention. It does, on the other hand, consider it necessary to consolidate the Framework Convention mechanism.[6]

With regard to the recommendation that a special instrument be prepared to protect immigrant communities, the Committee of Ministers would refer to the opinion of the Committee of Experts of the European Charter for Regional or Minority Languages (Appendix 3 of the current reply), without taking a position on the issue itself.[7]

With regard to the recommendation that the various sign languages used in Europe be given a protection similar to that afforded by the European Charter for Regional or Minority Languages, the Committee of Ministers takes note of the opinions of the Committee of Experts of the European Charter for Regional or Minority Languages and of the Committee on the Rehabilitation and Integration of People with disabilities (Partial Agreement) (CD-P-RR) (Appendix 3 and 4 respectively of the current reply)."[8]

Appendix 1

Opinion concerning Recommendation 1492 (2001) of the Parliamentary Assembly on the rights of national minorities

(Adopted by the CDDH during its 52nd meeting (6-9 November 2001))

1. The Steering Committee for Human Rights (CDDH) notes with interest Recommendation 1492 (2001) of the Parliamentary Assembly on the rights of national minorities, which is the subject of the present opinion. This opinion focuses on aspects of the recommendation which concern the CDDH's particular area of interest.

2. The CDDH agrees with the Assembly that the effective protection of the rights of minorities in Europe is essential to the implementation of fundamental human rights, stability, democratic security and peace on the continent. Together with the Assembly, it recognizes that this protection is an integral part of the protection of human rights. It also agrees that member states should show a more generous attitude in the implementation of Council of Europe instruments in the field of minorities, as these instruments set minimum standards only.

3. The CDDH refers to the opinion it gave on Recommendation 1345 (1997) of the Parliamentary Assembly on the protection of national minorities, the Final Declaration and the Action Plan of the Second Summit of Heads of State and Government of the Council of Europe (Strasbourg, 10-11 October 1997), the "Political Declaration adopted by Ministers of Council of Europe member states on Friday 13 October 2000 at the concluding session of the European Conference against Racism" and Resolution II "Respect for Human Rights, a Key Factor for Democratic Stability and Cohesion in Europe: Current Issues", adopted at the European Ministerial Conference on Human Rights (Rome, 3-4 November 2000) on the occasion of the 50th anniversary of the European Convention on Human Rights (4 November 2000).

Stepping up international co-operation
(see §12 (ii) of Recommendation 1492 (2001)

4. The CDDH agrees with the Assembly that it is necessary to further develop international co-operation in minority rights protection, both in their bilateral relations and at the level of European international organisations. It recalls that the Action Plan of the Second Summit of Heads of State and Government of the Council of Europe (Strasbourg, 10-11 October 1997) stated that "the Heads of State and Government, taking into account the imminent entry into force of the Framework Convention for the Protection of National Minorities, resolve to complement the Council of Europe's standard-setting achievements in this field through practical initiatives, such as confidence-building measures and enhanced co-operation, involving both governments and civil society".

5. It believes that intergovernmental co-operation activities are essential in this field. The CDDH therefore greatly regrets that the work of its Committee of Experts on Issues Relating to the Protection of National Minorities (DH-MIN) has been suspended since 2000 as the human and budgetary resources of the Secretariat had to be used urgently to rein-force those of the Advisory Committee on the Framework Convention. The DH-MIN had become an excellent forum for exchanging views, experiences and good practices, in order to favour the effective implementation of the international standards in this field. In addition, it always associated rep-resentatives of the civil society to its work. Consequently, the CDDH expresses the wish that financial and human resources be quickly made available to enable DH-MIN to resume its work.

6. The CDDH also takes note of the projects devised by the Council of Europe under the Stability Pact for South-Eastern Europe, and in particular three projects concerning national minorities (review of non-discrimination policies, accep-tance and implementation of existing norms and bilateral co-operation agreements), and the awareness-raising cam-

paign, "Link Diversity". These initiatives offer a new framework for the implementation of international co-operation. The CDDH also stresses that other co-operation activities are in progress (round tables, study visits and expert appraisals, especially on draft legislation concerning minorities). These activities are designed to raise awareness of the standards laid down in the Framework Convention for the Protection of National Minorities and to ensure that they are applied.

Increase in the number of states parties to the Framework Convention for the Protection of National Minorities, withdrawal of reservations and declarations
(see §12 (iii) (iv) of the Recommendation)

7. The aforementioned Ministerial Conference in Rome invited those member states which had not already done so to "consider or reconsider the possibility of becoming a Party to the Framework Convention for the Protection of National Minorities (1995) and the States Parties to co-operate fully with the monitoring mechanism set up by this Convention" (see paragraph 25 of Resolution II adopted by the Conference). The CDDH, which was instructed by the Ministers' Deputies on 10-11 January 2001 to implement several of the decisions taken at the Conference, intends to hold regular exchanges of views on the state of signatures and ratifications of the Framework Convention in order to encourage the states concerned to sign and/or ratify this convention as quickly as possible. In the absence of a definition of the notion national minority in the Framework Convention, the CDDH considered it useful to maintain the possibility for the Parties to this instrument to make reservations or declarations relating to the personal scope of the Framework Convention. Nevertheless, the CDDH shares the opinion of the Advisory Committee according to which, as regards reservations/declarations, the Parties to the Framework Convention should "exercise great restraint" (see § 6 of the opinion of the Advisory Committee on Recommendation 1492 (2001); document ACFC (2001) 3).

Increase in human and financial resources
(see §12 (vi) of the Recommendation)

8. Although this issue does not fall within its competence, the CDDH fully endorses the Parliamentary Assembly's proposal that human and financial resources should be increased to facilitate the implementation of the Framework Convention for the Protection of National Minorities.

Entry into force of Protocol No. 12 to the European Convention on Human Rights
(see §12 (vii) of the Recommendation)

9. When in force Protocol 12 should be such as to extend protection against all forms of discrimination and therefore, in the light of the interpretation given to it by the Court, help to improve certain aspects of protection of persons belonging to national minorities. The CDDH is keeping under close review the state of signatures and ratifications of the Protocol and regularly asks its members for an update.

Publication and dissemination of the work of the monitoring machinery set up within the Council of Europe
(see §12 (viii) of the Recommendation)

10. The CDDH is very interested to note that the Committee of Ministers has already started discussing the initial opinions of the Advisory Committee on the Framework Convention for the Protection of National Minorities. In this context, it warmly welcomes the steps taken by the Finnish, Hungarian, Liechtenstein and Slovak Governments to make these opinions public before the Committee of Ministers has even adopted its own conclusions and recommendations concerning them. The CDDH believes that this practice helps to encourage useful debate at national level on issues raised in these opinions, and that this example will be followed by the other States Parties to the Framework Convention, it being understood that states will first have had opportunity to address any inaccuracies. It also hopes that the period between the opinion of the Advisory Committee on the Framework Convention and the adoption of conclusions and

recommendations by the Committee of Ministers will be as short as possible.

11. The CDDH endorses the Parliamentary Assembly's proposal that there should be speedy publication and general dissemination of the results of the opinions and reports of the Advisory Committee on the Framework Convention for the Protection of National Minorities and of the Committee of Experts of the European Charter for Regional or Minority Languages. Public access to information in this field is a requirement of a pluralist, democratic society, as pointed out at the Ministerial Conference in Rome, and may be a force for democratic stability and cohesion in Europe.

12. The CDDH also points out that questions concerning national minorities are raised in the Council of Europe's human rights co-operation and awareness-raising programmes (information available on the Internet, information meetings in the countries concerned, etc).

Strengthening these mechanisms
(see §12 (ix) of the Recommendation)

13. The CDDH notes that the monitoring machinery initially set up by the Framework Convention for the Protection of National Minorities (Articles 24 to 26) has sometimes been thought too limited. It notes, however, that both the monitoring machinery and practice have expanded considerably since the adoption of the Framework Convention and are continuing to expand. It refers to Resolution (97) 10 ("Rules adopted by the Committee of Ministers on the Monitoring Arrangements under Articles 24 to 26 of the Framework Convention for the Protection of National Minorities"), adopted on 17 September 1997, to the Advisory Committee's Rules of Procedure, and to subsequent developments such as the practice of visits to countries and the authorisations adopted by the Committee of Ministers enabling the Advisory Committee to obtain information from other sources than governmental and to held meetings with such sources in the context of the visits, as well as the constructive dialogue that

developed between the Advisory Committee and the governments of Contracting Parties.

*Possible drafting of an additional protocol to the Framework
Convention*
(see §12 (x) of the Recommendation)

14. The CDDH notes the recommendation concerning the pos-
sible drafting, of an additional protocol to the Framework
Convention which would empower the European Court of
Human Rights, or a general Council of Europe judicial author-
ity, to give advisory opinions on the interpretation of this
Framework Convention.

15. The CDDH recognizes the existence of similarities between
some of the rights safeguarded by the Framework Convention
and other rights protected by the European Convention on
Human Rights,[9] but the nature of their respective provisions
are different: most of those contained in the Framework
Convention are programmatic provisions defining certain
objectives that the Parties undertake to pursue and that, in
principle at least, are not directly justiciable, as they imply that
the legislator, the government or the regional or local authorities take action. The Court recognizes quite openly this problem in paragraph 4 of the opinion it gave on 2 April 2001 on
Recommendation 1492 (2001), when questioning "whether
the interpretation of such provisions sits well with the judicial
function of the Court".[10]

16. The CDDH notes that the Court declares that it would in
principle be willing to undertake an interpretative role in this
field (see § 9 in the opinion of the Court). It underlines that this
role would be optional and that it could refrain from giving its
opinion, on a particular occasion, not only when an issue
could be considered non-justiciable but also "for other reasons" (id., § 6), which may possibly be linked to its judicial
function under the ECHR.[11]

17. For these reasons, the CDDH does not consider it advis-
able to envisage additional competences for the Court to be
laid down in an additional protocol. However, it considers it

necessary to consolidate the mechanism of the Framework Convention and the role of the Advisory Committee, including as regards the legal interpretation of the provisions of the Framework Convention.

Possible drafting of an additional protocol to the European Convention on Human Rights
(see §12 (xi) of the Recommendation)

18. The CDDH notes that the Parliamentary Assembly reiterates the proposals it made in Recommendation 1201 (1993) concerning an additional protocol on the rights of minorities to the European Convention on Human Rights. These proposals concerned, inter alia, the drafting of an additional protocol which would include the definition of national minority set out in Recommendation 1201 (1993).

19. The CDDH recalls that, at the First Summit of Heads of State and Government of the Council of Europe (Vienna, 8-9 October 1993), the Committee of Ministers was instructed "to begin work on drafting a protocol complementing the European Convention on Human Rights in the cultural field by provisions guaranteeing individual rights, in particular for persons belonging to national minorities". In January 1996, the Committee of Ministers decided to suspend the work on the elaboration of such an additional protocol, position which was reiterated in 1999, when it considered that the "approach to an additional protocol recommended by the Parliamentary Assembly, notably in Recommendation 1201, had proved not to be feasible for several reasons, inter alia because it contains certain elements (the definition of a national minority, the nature and scope of certain rights, etc) which do not muster the general support of all member states".[12] The Committee of Ministers added that its decision to suspend the work does not "imply a final decision on an additional protocol, but indeed leaves open the possibility of re-examining the question in the light of subsequent experience with the implementation of existing standards".

20. The CDDH believes that the reasons for this decision are still valid. It considers it somewhat premature to re-open dis-

133

cussions on the draft additional protocol proposed by the Parliamentary Assembly.

21. Finally, the CDDH points out that Article 1 of the afore-mentioned Protocol No. 12 to the European Convention on Human Rights stipulates that "the enjoyment of any right set forth by law shall be secured without discrimination on any ground such as sex, race, colour, language, religion, political or other opinion, national or social origin, association with a national minority, property, birth or other status". Consequently, once this additional protocol comes into force,[13] any discrimination against a person belonging to a national minority, including discrimination based on the fact that they belong to such a minority, would be covered by the general ban on discrimination.

Appendix 2

Opinion of the Advisory Committee on the Framework Convention for the Protection of National Minorities on Parliamentary Assembly Recommendation 1492 (2001) on the rights of national minorities

1. The Advisory Committee takes note with interest of the Parliamentary Assembly Recommendation 1492 (2001) on the rights of national minorities, which is the subject of this opinion. Being very closely concerned with most of the questions covered by Recommendation 1492, the Advisory Committee has examined the text carefully. This opinion is based on the discussions the Committee held on the matter at its 10th and 11th meetings.

2. Before making detailed comments on the various aspects of Recommendation 1492, the Advisory Committee wishes to join the Parliamentary Assembly in underlining the impor-tance of protecting the rights of national minorities in Europe effectively. As the only legally binding multilateral instrument that currently exists in Europe on the protection of national minorities in general, the Framework Convention is, in the Advisory Committee's view, the key tool for action in this area.

3. At the outset the Advisory Committee would like to emphasise that if the proposals formulated by the Parliamentary Assembly (in particular those mentioned under paragraph 12(x) and 12(xi)) are to be developed, it would be essential to initiate a substantial dialogue with many actors, including national minorities and other sectors of civil society.

*
* *

Further development of international co-operation
(see paragraph 12 (ii) of Recommendation 1492 (2001))

4. The Advisory Committee points out that the protection of national minorities is an integral component of the international protection of human rights and, as such, falls within the ambit of international co-operation. In addition, the Preamble of the Framework Convention recognises that the protection of national minorities is essential to the stability, democratic security and peace of our continent. The Advisory Committee therefore shares the Parliamentary Assembly's desire to improve and further develop international co-operation in this area. With regard to the bilateral relations referred to in the recommendation, it would point out that Article 2 of the Framework Convention specifically mentions the principles of good neighbourliness, friendly relations and co-operation between States, while Article 18 urges States to conclude bilateral and multilateral agreements and encourage transfrontier co-operation. This may also concern non-member States of the Council of Europe, as some of them are already Parties to the Framework Convention.

Increase in the number of States Parties to the Framework Convention for the Protection of National Minorities, revocation of reservations and declarations
(see paragraph 12 (iii), (iv) of Recommendation 1492 (2001))

5. The Advisory Committee supports the Parliamentary Assembly's proposal to ask those States which have not yet signed and/or ratified the Framework Convention to do so as

135

quickly as possible. It should be noted here that Belgium has signed the Framework Convention since Recommendation 1492 was adopted. As 34 States have ratified the Framework Convention and a further 8 States have signed but not yet ratified it, the Advisory Committee notes that the treaty now covers a very large geographical area and clearly embodies widely recognised standards for the protection of national minorities in Europe. It is therefore all the more important for the few member States that have not yet signed and/or ratified the Convention to do so and thus ensure that it applies in all Council of Europe member States in future.

6. With regard to the question of reservations and declarations to the Framework Convention, the Advisory Committee notes that, to a large extent, they pertain to the personal scope of application of the Framework Convention. In practice, certain States have adopted a more inclusive approach for the protection of national minorities in their policies and programmes than what is implied in their reservations and declarations (see related comments under paragraph 16). Bearing in mind the foregoing and the need to avoid undue restrictions on the scope of the Framework Convention, the Advisory Committee believes that States should exercise great restraint in making reservations/declarations when signing and/or ratifying the text. It also believes that States Parties should be encouraged to reconsider their reservations/declarations periodically with a view to possibly revoking them.

Ratification of the European Charter for Regional or Minority Languages
(see paragraph 12 (v) of Recommendation 1492 (2001))

7. Bearing in mind that the Framework Convention and the European Charter for Regional or Minority Languages may complement each other, the Advisory Committee shares the view that States that have not yet done so should be encouraged to ratify the Charter.

Increase in human and financial resources Strengthening of monitoring mechanisms
(see paragraph 12 (vi), (ix) of Recommendation 1492 (2001))

8. From the outset of its work, the Advisory Committee has felt that the resources allocated to it were inadequate in relation to the Committee's workload. This is principally the result of the rapid increase in the number of States Parties to the Framework Convention. While this increase is welcome, it obviously also has a major impact on the workload of the Advisory Committee and its secretariat, which is provided by the Directorate General of Human Rights. Notwithstanding certain improvements which the Advisory Committee acknowledged in its second activity report, the inadequacy of its resources is now, unfortunately, more acute than ever. The workload of the Advisory Committee and its secretariat is bound to increase significantly in the coming months and years. The Advisory Committee has now adopted 13 opinions and many more are under preparation. Furthermore the secretariat will need to provide important assistance to the Committee of Ministers so that the latter can carry out its task as the monitoring organ of the Framework Convention as effectively as possible.

9. Failure to find rapid solutions to these problems of resources could very quickly lead to delays in the presentation of the Advisory Committee's opinions and adoption of conclusions and recommendations by the Committee of Ministers and interfere with the operation of the monitoring mechanism as a whole. The Advisory Committee nevertheless believes that, given the way it has developed since the Framework Convention entered into force, the monitoring mechanism is perfectly capable of producing effective results provided that it is allocated adequate resources. The Advisory Committee therefore fully endorses the Parliamentary Assembly's proposal that the human and financial resources of the relevant departments should be increased and the monitoring mechanism strengthened. Already there have been serious concerns expressed on the major delays from the time of submitting the State report to the time of publish-

ing the respective opinion. These were expressed forcefully at a joint meeting of representatives of Governmental Offices for National Minorities and representatives of civil society in Strasbourg on 21 May 2001.

Signature and ratification of Protocol No. 12 to the European Convention on Human Rights
(see paragraph 12 (vii) of Recommendation 1492 (2001))

10. The Advisory Committee welcomes the Parliamentary Assembly's support for the signature and ratification of Protocol No. 12 to the European Convention on Human Rights. As efforts to combat discrimination are bound to help strengthen the protection of national minorities, the Advisory Committee hopes that Protocol No. 12 will enter into force as soon as possible.

Giving priority to discussion and adoption of the Advisory Committee's opinions
Establishing a suitable procedure for their prompt publication and general dissemination
(see paragraph 12 (viii) of Recommendation 1492 (2001))

11. As it has already explained on various occasions, in particular when its second activity report was presented to the Deputies, the Advisory Committee fully shares the Parliamentary Assembly's concern about the follow-up to its opinions. It believes that, in order to increase the effectiveness of its work and enable all interested parties, in particular at national level, to derive maximum benefit from the results of the monitoring procedure, it is essential that individual opinions be published as soon as possible after adoption, while they still have maximum impact. The Advisory Committee is therefore particularly pleased that, as noted by the Deputies at their 756th meeting, States Parties may, without prejudice to the Committee of Ministers' consideration of the opinion, publish the Advisory Committee's opinion concerning them, together with their own written comments, before the Committee of Ministers adopts its conclusions and any recommendations. The Advisory Committee notes with

satisfaction that Slovakia, Finland, Liechtenstein and Hungary have already taken advantage of this option and published, at an early stage, the opinions concerning them and their own comments, and hopes that other States Parties will follow their example. It believes that this practice is fully in line with the spirit of the Framework Convention, considering that the explanatory report provides that the monitoring of the implementation shall, in so far as possible, be transparent.

12. With regard to discussion of its opinions by the Deputies, the Advisory Committee observes that it is obviously the responsibility of the Committee of Ministers to determine its working methods for this phase in the monitoring process. The Advisory Committee has already said that it stands ready to be involved in some way in the exercise and possibly also in the follow-up to the Committee of Ministers' conclusions and recommendations. It therefore particularly appreciated being able, on 6 July 2001, at the first meeting of the GR-H devoted to examination of its opinions, to give a general presentation of the first four opinions adopted and reply to questions related to the opinions. The Advisory Committee attaches great importance to continuing and developing – as the Committee of Ministers considers the opinions submitted to it – the constructive dialogue between the two bodies involved in the monitoring of the Framework Convention. While reiterating its willingness to co-operate in this connection, the Advisory Committee also stresses that it is essential for the results of the monitoring process, i.e. its own opinions and the Committee of Ministers' conclusions/recommendations, to be available within a reasonable period of time. It therefore trusts that the Committee of Ministers will give the necessary priority to its work in this area, which is bound to strengthen the overall impact of the monitoring machinery.

Proposal to draft an additional protocol to the Framework Convention
(see paragraph 12 (x) of Recommendation 1492 (2001))

13. The Advisory Committee notes that the Parliamentary Assembly proposes that the Committee of Ministers begin

drafting a protocol to the Framework Convention giving the European Court of Human Rights or a general judicial authority of the Council of Europe the power to give advisory opinions concerning interpretation of the Framework Convention. The Advisory Committee points out that it had occasion to consider a similar proposal recently when asked for an opinion on the draft protocol to the Framework Convention presented by the Italian chairmanship of the Committee of Ministers (see documents CM (2000) 133 and 133 rev.). In its reply to the Chairman of the Ministers' Deputies on 10 January 2001, the Advisory Committee welcomed the aim of strengthening the Framework Convention and its monitoring mechanism, but noted that account should be taken of the fact that the mechanism was only now producing its first results as the Advisory Committee and the Committee of Ministers gained initial experiences of the procedure. It therefore felt that it was premature to alter the existing arrangements by introducing a new component such as that proposed in the draft protocol.

14. The Advisory Committee is still of the same opinion. In spite of having now adopted 13 opinions, it believes that it is still premature to alter the structure and functioning of the monitoring machinery under the Framework Convention. Not until the Committee of Ministers has adopted conclusions and possibly also recommendations concerning a significant number of countries and those countries have had some time to act upon them, including through an open debate at national level, will it be possible fully to assess the effectiveness – or shortcomings – of the monitoring machinery. It will be easier at that point to stand back and consider whether it is necessary to add to the machinery in the manner recommended by the Parliamentary Assembly.

Proposal to draft an additional protocol to the European Convention on Human Rights
(see paragraph 12 (xi) of Recommendation 1492 (2001))

15. The Advisory Committee notes that the Parliamentary Assembly proposes that the Committee of Ministers begin

drafting an additional protocol to the European Convention on Human Rights, drawing on the principles contained in Recommendation 1201 (1993), and endeavouring to include therein the definition of national minority adopted in the same recommendation. The Advisory Committee is in favour of initiatives intended to strengthen further the international legal standards aimed at the protection of national minorities and, in principle, it welcomes the aim of the present initiative. At the same time, the Advisory Committee recalls that the question of a protocol complementing the European Convention on Human Rights in the cultural field by provisions guaranteeing individual rights, in particular for persons belonging to national minorities, was discussed in detail by the member States of the Council of Europe and that due to difficulties in reaching a consensus on the issues concerned, work on this initiative was suspended.

16. As concerns the issue of including a definition of the term national minority in such an instrument, the Advisory Committee is of the opinion that it would be likely to have an impact on the implementation of the Framework Convention. Bearing in mind reservations and declarations formulated by States Parties (see related comments under paragraph 6), there is a risk that such a definition would reflect only the lowest common denominator, which could have implications on the scope of application of the Framework Convention and have the effect of depriving certain minorities of the protection that the Framework Convention offers. At the same time, the Advisory Committee notes that certain States have taken advantage of the flexibility offered by the Framework Convention by adopting a very inclusive approach to the question of the personal scope of application of the Framework Convention.

17. In the Advisory Committee's opinion, the Framework Convention is not an instrument that operates on an "all-or-nothing" basis. Even if a group is covered by the Framework Convention, it does not necessarily follow that all of the Convention's articles apply to the persons belonging to that minority. Similarly, if a minority is not covered by the major-

ity of the provisions in the Framework Convention, that does not necessarily mean that none of the provisions is relevant to the members of that group. The Advisory Committee believes that a nuanced, article-by-article approach to the "definition" question is not only fully in line with the text of the Framework Convention but is actually dictated by it. This flexibility in the implementation of the Framework Convention could be made more difficult by including a definition in a legally binding European instrument.

Attaching to the Commissioner for Human Rights a person with special responsibility for issues concerning the protection of minorities' rights
(see paragraph 12 (xii) of Recommendation 1492 (2001))

18. Bearing in mind that the protection of national minorities is an integral part of the international protection of human rights, and without commenting on whether a person with special responsibility for issues concerning the protection of the rights of minorities should be attached to the Commissioner for Human Rights, the Advisory Committee strongly believes that it is important to undertake further efforts to dovetail the work of the Commissioner for Human Rights and that of the other bodies of the Council of Europe that play a role in protecting national minorities and create synergies between them.

Appendix 3

Opinion of the Committee of Experts of the European Charter for Regional or Minority Languages on Recommendation 1492 of the Parliamentary Assembly on the Rights of National Minorities

The Committee of Experts of the European Charter for Regional or Minority Languages has taken note of the invitation of the Committee of Ministers to give its opinion on Recommendation 1492 of the Parliamentary Assembly on Rights of National Minorities, and in particular on its paragraphs 12 (xiii) and (xiv).

142

As a body of independent experts established on the basis of the Charter for the purpose of monitoring the application of the Charter by the Parties, the Committee has restricted its observations to matters having a direct bearing on its own field of competence.

*

*   *

The Committee of Experts underlines the importance of the Charter for preserving and promoting regional or minority languages in Europe. Since the success of the Charter depends largely on the commitment of European states with regard to its ratification and implementation, the Committee notes with satisfaction the encouragement given to this end by paragraph 12 (v) of the Assembly Recommendation. It welcomes the recent ratifications by Denmark, Slovenia, the United Kingdom and Spain and emphasises the need for other Council of Europe member states to increase their momentum in the preparation of ratification.

With regard to the specific recommendations contained in paragraphs 11 and 12 (xiii) of the Assembly Recommendation, the Committee of Experts points out that the protection provided by the Charter is specifically designed for those languages defined in its Article 1, that is languages that are "traditionally used within a given territory of a State by nationals of that State..." and "different from the official language(s) of the State". It does not include the dialects of the official language(s) and the languages of migrants. The Charter may also be applied to less widely used official languages (Article 3). Thus the authors of the Charter, in adopting these formulations, limited the application of the Charter to certain categories of languages.

This limitation by no means implies that the languages of migrants or sign languages should not receive an appropriate form of protection. With regard to the former, the authors of the Charter considered that the nature of the questions raised by the situation of migrants merited a specific protection and that their languages should be treated separately, if appropriate in a specific legal instrument (cf. Explanatory Report, paragraph 15). The Committee endorses this view. It also wishes to point out that, although the history and needs of these languages are indeed different from those covered by the Charter, with the passage of time the languages of immigrants may become "traditionally used within a given territory of a State".

As for sign languages, it must be recognised that the Charter was not conceived to meet their specific needs. Sign languages are present in all European states and they are not at present the subject of a special international instrument addressing their particular needs, whether from a social, cultural or human rights perspective. The Committee of Experts would welcome an initiative aiming to promote and protect sign languages through a separate instrument that would take into account the special situation and needs of the users of these languages.

With regard to paragraph 12 (viii) and (xiv) of Recommendation 1492, the Committee of Experts underlines that the monitoring mechanism of the Charter is the key to its successful application. Having adopted its first reports on the application of the Charter in Croatia, Hungary, Liechtenstein, Finland and the Netherlands, Norway and Switzerland, the Committee strongly endorses the Assembly's call for the Committee of Ministers to make these reports public, especially in the light of the Council of Europe's policy in favour of transparency.

The Committee of Experts welcomes the Assembly's recommendations in paragraphs 12 (vi) and (ix) concerning the strengthening of the monitoring mechanisms and the need to increase the human and financial resources of the directorate general of the Council of Europe concerned by the application of the Charter.

The Committee has noted that, by comparison with other convention mechanisms, the budget of the European Charter for Regional or Minority Languages is extremely modest. Moreover, with the growing number of Parties to the Charter,

144

the workload and the financial implications of the Charter are also increasing. As a result, increased resources will be needed to make provision for:

- more members of the Committee (the current tally of 13 members could reach about 17 in 2002);
- more meeting days to cope with the workload generated by the review of national reports;
- more "on-the-spot visits" to States Parties, which have proved indispensable in order to obtain a clear view of the situation;
- increased costs for translation of documents,

as well as to finance information seminars and technical assistance to promote understanding of the Charter and assist with the preparation of well-conceived instruments of ratification. For the same reasons, the present secretarial team of two administrators and one assistant is becoming increasingly overburdened and will need to be reinforced.

The Committee of Experts considers that if its budget is not adapted to the mission given to the Committee in accordance with the Charter, this will have a serious effect on its ability to maintain the quality of its work. It therefore shares the opinion of the Parliamentary Assembly that it is necessary for the Committee of Ministers to take into account the financial and human resources needed to ensure the successful functioning of the monitoring mechanism.

Appendix 4

Committee on the Rehabilitation and Integration of People with disabilities (Partial Agreement)(CD-P-RR)

Opinion on Parliamentary Assembly Recommendation 1492 (2001) on the Rights of National Minorities (in particular paragraph 12.xiii on sign languages)

1. *Recommendation 1492 (2001)* on the rights of national minorities was adopted by the Parliamentary Assembly of the Council of Europe on 23 January 2001. It was examined by the Ministers' Deputies at the 742nd meeting (15 February 2001),

145

who decided, on that occasion, to assign ad hoc terms of reference to the Committee on the Rehabilitation and Integration of People with disabilities (Partial Agreement) (CD-P-RR) inviting it to draw up an opinion on that Recommendation, in particular paragraph 12. xiii, and to submit this opinion to the Committee of Ministers by 31 December 2001 (Decision No. CM/775/15022001).

2. *In paragraph 12.* xiii the Parliamentary Assembly recommends that the Committee of Ministers "give the various sign languages utilised in Europe a protection similar to that afforded by the European Charter for Regional or Minority Languages, possibly by means of the adoption of a recommendation to member states."

3. *Full citizenship.* In response to the Committee of Ministers' request, the CD-P-RR has carefully studied Recommendation 1492 (2001) and would like to emphasize that the general philosophy on which the recommendation is based, namely the protection of the rights of minorities, and subsequently the integration of these minorities, is very much in keeping with the committee's own approach towards social cohesion, namely to promote equal opportunities, independent living, full citizenship and active participation of people with disabilities in the life of the community.

4. *Protection, promotion and recognition.* Consequently, the Committee wishes to point out that it shares the Assembly's concerns and considers that due protection and recognition should be given to sign languages, and that their use should be promoted. Sign language is a vital means of communication for many people who have a hearing disability. An improved status, meaning the recognition and legal anchoring of sign languages should result in better social integration of people with a hearing impairment. In addition, a formal recognition possibly increases the provision of sign language interpreters. Furthermore, it wishes to stress that it supports the views expressed on this issue in the opinion of the Committee of Experts of the European Charter for Regional or

Minority Languages on Recommendation 1492 of the Parliamentary Assembly (Doc. MIN-LANG (2001) 9).

5. *Sign languages are not universal.* "Sign language" is often used as a generic term to refer to one specific sign language, e.g. British Sign Language (BSL), or to refer to the whole language family: "sign languages" as opposed to "spoken languages". In reality, there may be just as many sign languages as there are spoken indigenous languages, whose current number is estimated at more than 200 in Europe, and maybe more than 6000 worldwide. And many of them are mutually unintelligible (just as much as spoken languages).

6. *Sign languages are full natural languages.* In line with the European Parliament Resolution on sign languages for the deaf of 17 June 1988, the CD-P-RR considers that sign languages are languages in their own right, and that they are the preferred or only language of large numbers of deaf people. Sign languages are not the same as sign systems. They employ structural and functional properties common to all natural languages. Like any other languages they consist of an arbitrary system of symbols used to communicate, convey social relationships, express cultural identity, and to provide a source of delight through artistic forms of expression (literature, drama, comedy, poetry). Signed sentences are true sentences with both noun and verb components. Sign languages have their own vocabulary/lexicon of thousands of words, and a grammar (word formation, sentence construction, tenses, active-passive) as complex as spoken languages. However, they are not derived from spoken languages but developed gradually and naturally as mother tongues among the deaf communities.[14] Consequently, there is very little similarity between American Sign Language (ASL), British Sign Language (BSL) and Irish Sign Language (ISL), since the deaf communities are independent of each other. Since sign languages have developed historically, like other natural languages, they are not to be confused with invented systems, such as Esperanto for example. Sign languages use tropes (metaphors, similes, metonomy). There are regional, social, ethnic, age-related, gender-specific and register variations.

There are identifiable age-appropriate developmental phases in the language acquisition process. All characteristics of sign languages can be studied within the relevant linguistic sub-disciplines, such as phonology, morphology, lexicology, syntax, semantics, pragmatics, socio-linguistics, etc.

7. *Sign language users form a minority.* In keeping with the same European Parliament resolution, the CD-P-RR considers that sign languages are the preferred or only language of large numbers of deaf people.[15] It has been estimated that the ratio of pre-lingually deaf persons is approximately 1 in 1000. However, since also post-lingually deaf persons, families of deaf children, teachers, social workers, etc. need to use sign languages, the number of sign language users is considerably larger than the number of deaf persons. Sign language users are a minority, since they are a group numerically inferior to the rest of the population of a state, in a non-dominant position, possessing linguistic characteristics differing from those of the rest of the population and show, if only implicitly, a sense of solidarity, directed towards preserving what constitutes their common identity, including their culture, traditions and language (cf the proposed definition of "national minority" in Parliamentary Assembly Recommendation 1201 (1993)). Both Finland and Portugal have already enshrined the rights of sign languages users in their constitutions.

8. *Sign languages as non-territorial languages.* Sign languages can, in principle, be regarded as non-territorial languages. It is pertinent to note that sign languages meet the definition criteria of non-territorial languages as set out in the European Charter for Minority or Regional Languages, i.e. "Languages used by nationals of the state which differ from the language or languages used by the rest of the state's population but which, although traditionally used within the territory of the state, cannot be identified with a particular area thereof" (Part I, Article 1c.) Sign languages are typically used throughout the country of which they are native: British Sign Language in Great Britain, French Sign Language in France, German Sign Language in Germany, Italian Sign Language in Italy, etc. However, it is worth noting that in some countries

more than one sign language may exist. These sign languages are used in certain geographical areas only and thus meet the definition of regional minority languages. For example: In Spain, Catalonian Sign Language is used in Catalonia, and Galician Sign Language in Galicia; in Belgium, Flemish Belgian Sign Language, Belgian French Sign Language, and German Sign Language are used; in Switzerland, Swiss-German, Swiss-French and Swiss-Italian Sign Language(s) are used; in Finland, Finnish Sign Language and Finnish-Swedish Sign Language are used.

9. *Sign languages and linguistic and cultural diversity.* Sign language users are a cultural and linguistic minority. In relation to the European Parliament Resolution on sign languages of 18 November 1998, the CD-P-RR considers that every one of the different sign languages used in Europe has its specific cultural identity. In accordance with the Council of Europe Declaration on cultural diversity, adopted by the Committee of Ministers on 7 December 2000, member states should develop and/or maintain measures to sustain, protect and promote linguistic and cultural diversity, in order to enhance pluralism and multi-cultural societies in Europe. Also sign languages should be recognised as an expression of cultural wealth. They constitute an important element of Europe's linguistic and cultural heritage.

10. *Aims and principles.* The design of any instrument or policy to protect and promote sign languages and the rights of their users should be preceded by the establishment of clear aims, guiding principles, definite time frames, reasonable targets, resources and methods used, based on a thorough needs analysis Users should participate in this process as early as possible.

11. *Prohibition of all forms of unjustified distinction, restriction, or exclusion.* Deaf and hearing impaired persons have the right to accessible and suitable communication, by means of reasonable adjustment particularly in the fields of:

– education, incl. higher education,

– cultural activities (artistic productions), religion, and media,

149

- economic/vocational integration,
- social integration (e.g. transport, political participation),
- legal/judicial or other public authorities, administrations or
- public services (e.g. health care, including mental health, social services such as family counselling services).

Most countries have mounted programmes and activities to support sign languages, but have also encountered difficulties in their implementation. One of the most striking obstacles is the shortage of sign language interpreters.

Specific measures could include the provision of appropriate forms and means of/for:

- Training of sign language interpreters and tutors (official recognition as a profession, recognised qualifications, full-time training);
- Training of mother tongue sign language users to become teachers, and training of teachers who are not native sign-ers to acquire sign language skills similar to native signer standards.
- Teaching sign languages to hearing children, adults, family members, and persons who work with deaf people.
- Providing television programmes accessible to deaf people (subtitling, sign language interpretation).
- Providing harmonised text telephone and videophone systems (universal design/design for all). In this context the CD-P-RR would like to draw attention to Resolution ResAP(2001)3 "Towards full citizenship for people with disabilities through inclusive new technologies", adopted by the Committee of Ministers on 24 October 2001.
- Deaf awareness training.
- Promoting research.
- Creation or nomination of centres of excellence.
- Creation of university chairs.
- Publication of multilingual sign language dictionaries.
- Exchange of information, also at international level.

aiming at effectiveness and cost-effectiveness as genuine guiding principles of fair and democratic societies, in order to arrive at a real improvement in the present situation.

13. *Council of Europe meetings.* Furthermore, the CD-P-RR calls on the Committee of Ministers to ensure that meetings organised by the Council of Europe are accessible to deaf people by providing sign languages interpretation services on request.

14. *New technologies – a cure against deafness?* The use of sign languages cannot yet be fully replaced by technical aids. The CD-P-RR would like to draw attention to its report "Cochlear Implants in Deaf Children", published in May 2001, which compares current cochlear implantation policy and practice in 10 European countries, analysing in particular ethical aspects as well as the psychological and social consequences in deaf children. The study concludes that, despite cochlear implantations, pre-lingually deaf children will not become "normal" hearing children. They will be able to perceive sounds from the environment, including most speech sounds. But to hear speech sounds does not mean to understand spoken language. Children with a cochlear implant will thus always be at a disadvantage in aural/oral communication processes. Consequently, the report recommends to combine cochlear implantation with the teaching and learning of sign languages.

15. *Report on the status of sign languages.* Concerning the official recognition of sign languages at national level the CD-P-RR could consider drafting a report for the attention of the Parliamentary Assembly on the status of sign languages in member states.

16. *In conclusion,* and without prejudice to the foregoing comments, the CD-P-RR welcomes the Parliamentary Assembly Recommendation as a further substantial step in securing human rights and dignity, full citizenship and active participation in the life of the community for all people with disabilities. Pursuant to the Flensburg Recommendations on the implementation of policy measures for regional or minority

151

languages, issued by the European Centre for Minority Issues (ECMI) in June 2000, the CD-P-RR recommends that the Council of Europe should prepare a legal instrument to safeguard sign languages and the rights of their users and in particular to promote the individual right to the general use of sign languages and facilitating that use by a co-ordinated set of measures deemed most appropriate, reflecting the variety of instruments, policies and practices in member states. In this connection, some delegations expressed themselves in favour of recommending the elaboration of an additional protocol on sign languages to the European Charter for Regional or Minority Languages.

Appendix 5

Opinion of the Commissioner for Human Rights on Recommendation 1492 (2001) of the Parliamentary Assembly on rights of national minorities

In my capacity as Commissioner for Human Rights I share the Parliamentary Assembly's view on the need for Member States to guarantee sufficient protection for national minorities to enable them to contribute, alongside the majority, to the social cohesion and democratic pluralism of the nation.

For my part, I make every effort, during my visits to member States, to contact those minorities who wish to inform me of their difficulties. The reports I have transmitted to the Committee of Ministers and the Parliamentary Assembly contain, moreover, a number of recommendations specifically related to certain national minorities.

Having regard to the proposal of the Assembly to place an agent specifically concerned with the protection of the rights of minorities in my office, I am obliged to stress that, since taking up my functions in 1999, the very small number of permanent A grade agents in my office, at present only three, barely enables me to accomplish all the tasks expected of me by my mandate.

This being so, any reinforcement of my office by the placement of an additional permanent agent would be welcome, it being understood that this agent would be called on to deal not only with minority problems but, when necessary, to contribute also to the other activities of my office.

Appendix 6

Opinion of the European Court of Human Rights on the Draft Additional Protocol to the Framework Convention for the Protection of National Minorities (on the interpretation of the Convention)

(Adopted at its plenary administrative meeting on 2 April 2001)

1. At their meeting on 30 October 2000 the Ministers' Deputies decided to transmit to the European Court of Human Rights the text of a draft Protocol to the Framework Convention for the Protection of National Minorities conferring competence on the European Court of Human Rights to give advisory opinions concerning the interpretation of the Framework Convention.

2. In response to that request the Court wishes firstly to stress the importance of the protection of minorities. It welcomes the progress that has been made in that field under the auspices of the Council of Europe. The Framework Convention for the Protection of National Minorities is an important milestone in this regard. The object and purpose of the Framework Convention is wholly in keeping with the philosophy of the European Convention on Human Rights, to which the former makes express reference (the preamble and Articles 19 and 23, see paragraph 3 below).

3. There is considerable common ground between the two instruments, not only in terms of the substantive rights and freedoms enshrined in the Framework Convention (see notably Articles 7 to 9), but also in respect of the permitted limitations (Article 19 - limitations only as provided for in particular in the Human Rights Convention) and the determination of the scope of rights and freedoms (Article 23 – rights and freedoms enshrined in the Framework Convention to be

understood as conforming to the corresponding Human Rights Convention provisions).

4. The Court notes that its proposed role in the interpretation of the Framework Convention would only be supplementary to that of the Committee of Ministers and the Advisory Committee established under Article 26 of the Framework Convention. According to the Italian Chair's explanatory note, the main purpose of the proposed Protocol is to reinforce this Committee (CM(2000)133 rev). The Court does indeed consider that the clarification of the content of the type of obligation provided for in the Framework Convention may be best achieved through a process of dialogue between the Contracting States and the Committee of Ministers, assisted by the Advisory Committee. In this connection it recalls that, unlike the Human Rights Convention which sets forth immediately binding obligations, the Framework Convention was intended to contain "mostly programme-type provisions setting out objectives which the parties undertake to pursue" and which are not "directly applicable". (Framework Convention for the Protection of National Minorities: Explanatory Report, paragraph 11). It might be questioned whether the interpretation of such provisions sits well with the judicial function of the Court.

5. However, particularly in view of the need to avoid divergent interpretation of the concepts common to both instruments and having regard to the supplementary character of the role envisaged by the additional Protocol, the Court is willing to assume the task assigned to it under the draft Protocol to the extent that this is compatible with its judicial function.

6. In this connection the Court notes that its strictly judicial role has been taken into account in the draft in so far as the word "may" in Article 1 of the draft Protocol is intended to imply the possibility (which exists in any case) for the Court to refrain from giving its opinion on a particular occasion. The Court might feel the need for restraint not only in order to cope with the possibility of questions considered to be non-justiciable, but also for other reasons. In this regard reference

can be made to the Court's power to give advisory opinions under Article 47 of the European Convention on Human Rights (also mentioned in the proposal by the Italian Chair). According to paragraph 2 of that Article, such opinions shall not deal, inter alia, with any questions which the Court might be called upon to consider in connection with individual cases before it. On similar grounds the Court might feel unable to give an advisory opinion on the Framework Convention, if the request relates to provisions directly corresponding to guarantees set out in the Human Rights Convention. The possibility of such situations arising may be increased by the forthcoming entry into force of Protocol No. 12 to the European Convention on Human Rights containing a general prohibition of discrimination.

7. The Court further observes that draft Article 1 is modeled on Article 29 of the Convention on Human Rights and Biomedicine. It provides: "The European Court of Human Rights may give, without direct reference to any specific proceedings pending in a court..." This wording should be seen in light of the fact that the Convention on Human Rights and Biomedicine was expected to be applied by domestic courts. As the Framework Convention, on the other hand, is not intended to be directly applicable in this way, the situations in which the Court would have to refrain from giving an advisory opinion (or limit its scope) because of pending national proceedings, are likely to arise very rarely. The Court therefore considers that a reference to such proceedings as the only example of circumstances in which the giving of an advisory opinion might not be proper is not appropriate in the context of the Framework Convention. Instead, the words underlined above could be replaced by a more general wording indicating that the new power to give advisory opinions is without prejudice to the Court's judicial function. The first sub-paragraph of paragraph 1 of the proposed new Article 27 could therefore read as follows:

"The European Court of Human Rights may give, in so far as this does not prejudice the exercise of its judicial function, advisory

155

opinions on legal questions concerning the interpretation of the present Convention at the request of: ..."

8. Finally, although it is not likely that the entry into force of the proposed protocol would alone lead to a dramatic increase in the Court's workload, it would add another new task for the Court. This should be taken into account in medium- and long-term planning and provision for the Court and the Convention system.

9. In conclusion, and without prejudice to the foregoing comments, the Court is in principle willing to assume an interpretative role in the field of minority protection as envisaged in the draft Additional Protocol to the Framework Convention for the Protection of National Minorities.

Notes

1 See paragraph 12.i and ii of Parliamentary Assembly Recommendation 1492.

2 See paragraph 12.iii, iv, v and vii of Parliamentary Assembly Recommendation 1492.

3 See paragraph 12.viii and xiv of Parliamentary Assembly Recommendation 1492.

4 See paragraph 12.vi, ix and xii of Parliamentary Assembly Recommendation 1492.

5 See paragraph 12.xi of Parliamentary Assembly Recommendation 1492.

6 See paragraph 12.x of Parliamentary Assembly Recommendation 1492.

7 See paragraph 11 of Parliamentary Assembly Recommendation 1492.

8 See paragraph 12.xiii of Parliamentary Assembly Recommendation 1492.

9 The CDDH recalls in this respect Article 23 of the Framework Convention according to which "the rights and freedoms flowing from the principles enshrined in the present framework Convention, in so far as they are subject of a corresponding provision in the Convention for the Protection of Human Rights and Fundamental Freedoms, or in the Protocols thereto, shall be understood so as to conform to the latter provisions".

10 See the Opinion of the European Court of Human Rights on the Draft Additional Protocol to the Framework Convention for the Protection of National Minorities (on the interpretation of the Convention) adopted during the plenary administrative session held on 2 April 2001, § 4.

11 In this respect the CDDH the proposal for an amendment made by the Italian authorities on 13 September 2001 aiming at specifying in the text of the draft additional protocol to the Framework Convention that the Court's role of interpreting should apply "in so far as this does not prejudice the exercise of its judicial function."

12 See the decision adopted by the Ministers' Deputies at their 656th meeting on 19 January 1999, item 4.1.

13 Opened for signature by Council of Europe member states on 4 November 2000 (at 24 July 2001, one state had ratified the additional protocol and 26 had signed it).

14 Some linguists even argue that gesture-based sign languages preceded spoken languages in the evolutionary process. See William C. Stokoe, Language in Hand: Why Sign came before Speech, Gallaudet University Press 2001.

15 There is no common definition of "deafness" in Europe. However, as a general indication, "deafness" is defined in many countries as a hearing loss of 80dB. For a comparative analysis of criteria see the Council of Europe publication "Assessing Disability in Europe – Similarities and Differences (2002).

APPENDIX III

Recommendation 1598 (2003) of the Parliamentary Assembly of the Council of Europe "Protection of sign languages in the member states of the Council of Europe"[1]

1. The Parliamentary Assembly recalls its Recommendation 1492 (2001) on the rights of national minorities, and particularly paragraph 12.xiii concerning sign languages.

2. The Assembly takes note of the reply by the Committee of Ministers to this recommendation, contained in Document 9492. It regrets that the Committee of Ministers did not make a pronouncement on the opinions delivered by the Committee of Experts of the European Charter for Regional or Minority Languages (ETS No. 148) and by the Committee on the Rehabilitation and Integration of People with disabilities (Partial Agreement). This reply warrants, if any justification were needed, the Parliamentary Assembly's concern that the rights of sign language users should be incorporated into a specific legal instrument, or into an additional protocol to the charter, without prejudging the position that may be adopted by the organisations representing deaf people.

---

1. *Assembly debate* on 1 April 2003 (11th Sitting) (see Doc. 9738, report of the Committee on Legal Affairs and Human Rights, rapporteur: Mr Bruce; and Doc. 9765, opinion of the Social, Health and Family Affairs Committee, rapporteur: Baroness Knight).
Text adopted by the Assembly on 1 April 2003 (11th Sitting).

3. The Assembly recognises sign languages as the expression of Europe's cultural wealth. They are a feature of Europe's linguistic and cultural heritage.

4. The Assembly also recognises sign languages as a complete and natural means of communication for deaf people.

5. The Assembly takes the view that official recognition of these languages will help deaf people to become integrated into society and gain access to justice, education and employment.

6. The Assembly acknowledges the importance of a detailed study of requirements, necessarily preceding the framing of any policy on sign languages. It stresses the need to involve users of these languages in the process.

7. The Assembly observes that a number of member states have introduced programmes in support of sign languages. Although all experience a shortage of sign language interpreters, this demonstrates the strength of demand and the positive and inclusive social benefits such services provide.

8. The Assembly takes the view that official recognition of sign languages will facilitate the training, recruitment and retention of more interpreters.

9. For the above reasons, and in the knowledge that only action at European level will afford a solution to this problem, the Assembly recommends that the Committee of Ministers devise a specific legal instrument on the rights of sign language users, and accordingly:

i. instruct the relevant bodies of the Council of Europe to undertake a preparatory study in consultation with national experts and representatives of the deaf community in order to clarify outstanding issues in regard to the protection of the use of sign languages;

ii. define clear goals to be achieved, exact deadlines to be met, and resources and methods to be used, founded on a full study of requirements with the mandatory participation of associations representing the users of these languages;

iii. consider drafting an additional protocol to the European Charter for Regional or Minority Languages incorporating sign languages into the charter, among the non-territorial minority languages.

10. The Assembly also recommends that the Committee of Ministers encourage member states:

i.   to give the sign languages used in their territory formal recognition;

ii.   to train sign language interpreters and sign language tutors;

iii. to give education in sign languages to deaf people;

iv.   to train teachers, in preparation for working with deaf and hearing-impaired children, in sign languages;

v.   to broadcast television programmes in sign languages, and make sign language subtitling of programmes transmitted in spoken language a general practice;

vi.   to inform deaf and hearing-impaired people about the use of sign languages;

vii. to utilise the new technologies and make them available to deaf people;

viii. to include sign languages as a valid academic qualification in mainstream secondary schools with equal status to other taught languages;

ix.   to grant deaf people the right to choose freely between oral and bilingual school systems;

x.   to subsidise the publication of instructive literature in sign languages.

APPENDIX IV

(Adopted by the Deputies on 16 June 2004 at their 888th meeting)

Reply of the Committee of Ministers of the Council of Europe to Parliamentary Assembly Recommendation 1598 (2003)

1.   The Committee of Ministers has been paying sustained attention to the question concerning the protection of sign languages and the rights of their users since the adoption of its reply to Parliamentary Assembly Recommendation 1492 (2001) on the rights of national minorities, which contained a paragraph on sign languages, and, more particularly since the Assembly's Recommendation 1598 (2003) on protection of sign languages in the member states of the Council of Europe.

2.   On receipt of this recommendation, the Committee of Ministers requested three Council of Europe expert committees, namely in the fields of education, rehabilitation of disabled people and protection of regional/minority languages, to give their opinions on it.

3.   On the basis of these opinions, the relevant Committee of Ministers subsidiary bodies held in-depth discussions and the following conclusions were reached:

a. sign languages are important and merit special consideration and protection;

b. the action of the Council of Europe should be focused more on access to rights by the users of sign languages than on promoting the status of the language;

c. before deciding on the question of any possible future instrument, a study of the needs of sign language users, including consultation with sign language users and organisations representing them, should be conducted.

4. The Committee of Ministers welcomes the idea of holding an international conference on sign languages, under the aegis of the Council of Europe, with the participation of sign language users in due course, depending on resources available. The Parliamentary Assembly would be invited to be represented at any such Conference.

5. The Committee of Ministers considers that, in line with item 9.i. of the recommendation, such a conference could be instrumental in clarifying outstanding issues and moving the agenda forward.

6. A study of the current situation in respect of sign languages and the rights of their users in a number of member states, presently conducted by the Council of Europe, could serve as a starting point for the above-mentioned needs analysis.

7. The Committee of Ministers will inform the Assembly on further development in this regard.

Sales agents for publications of the Council of Europe
Agents de vente des publications du Conseil de l'Europe